Everyday play is fabulous!
(written with my left hand)

CORNELIA PARKER

EVERYDAY PLAY

INSANITY

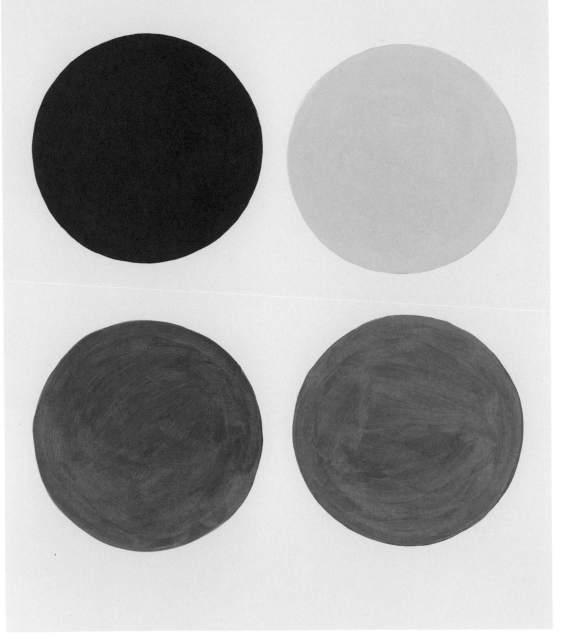

David Shrigley, *Insanity*, 2014

EVERYDAY PLAY

edited by julian rothenstein

foreword by andrey kurkov

A REDSTONE BOOK

CONTENTS

FOREWORD BY ANDREY KURKOV

British kings and queens and Russian tzars refer to themselves in speeches as 'We'. They do not hide their plurality. On the contrary, they project it, possibly not always understanding that this we, which they attach to themselves, almost certainly contains a more serious and weighty truth than one might think. Yes, royalty cannot refer to itself simply as 'I'. That would be too shallow and restricting. The king or queen is We: that is, each of them is a separate we. But in fact, we, used in this way – only for the sake of an external ritual to project one's image – humiliates this important personal pronoun and hides the ordinary, daily drama it carries in itself, especially when a person addresses himself or herself as we quite consciously and intentionally. In fact, each of us, and certainly each reader of this book, is a person who understands that he or she is not really he or she at all, but they. Or, to put it more simply, each reader of this book is we: a two-eyed, two-eared, one-nosed, two-armed and two-legged we. Why? Because only the simplest individual, absolutely deprived of education or reading, can remain an I. A person who has absorbed any knowledge of the world is automatically multiplied from within, accommodating the thoughts and feelings of others in his or her thoughts and feelings, and becoming enriched with knowledge or ideas, some of which enter a person together with their creators or the best propagandists of those ideas.

Eric Satie, Peter the Great, Marcel Proust, John Baldessari, Luis Buñuel, Velimir Khlebnikov and many others shared personal secrets that can turn the inner world of each of us upside down. The visual unexpectedness and the paradoxical nature of this book may well make you reach for some soothing eye drops. But once you have applied the drops, I would recommend that you take another close look. The visuals are worth it! And one more thing: Don't try to read this book in one go!

In my Soviet kindergarten, I was told a great deal about Vladimir Lenin – Grandfather Lenin – so much, that he still lives somewhere in me. I remember his family, and how after a meal it was customary for them to lick their plates so that not a scrap of food was left. To further their waste-not-want-not principle, Lenin's parents even invented for their children the Society of Clean Plates! Having ingested Lenin, I went on to the father of

Russian absurdist literature, Daniil Kharms. First, I let in his poems and short stories, filled with black humour; and then he himself squeezed through and hid in the depths of my being. Yes, I do know that he died of starvation in a psychiatric asylum in the besieged city of Leningrad, in February 1942. But I also know that crazy people don't die! They just reincarnate as other madmen, while partially hiding inside normal people. Normal people are those who can say we about themselves. Because only a person who is painfully modest or completely uneducated would say I.

If I smoked, I would smoke a pipe and hold it the way Hemingway did.

But I don't smoke. That is, we do not smoke. We prefer to drink. We drink whisky and play Scrabble. We do not know yet which of the great or the strange loved to drink whisky and play Scrabble, coming up with new words as they went along. If no such character has yet been identified – I will be the first. Sorry – *we* will be the first! By the way, do you know how to introduce new words into the world of old words? Very simple! Write a new word online and the meaning you give it. Preferably several times, paraphrasing the definition. Then ask Google a question about this word, and if Google directs you to your post, the word is accepted.

This is a fascinating book. It fascinated me/us so much that I/we tried out many of the strange games, habits, rituals and principles described in it and also chose several heroes of the book for personal experiments. I/we wish you the joy of doing the same!

Read on! It will not be boring! It will be fun and thought provoking! Certainly, you will acquire some new recipes for life. After all, the well-prepared life of someone else is bound to bring on a healthy feeling of hunger as well as a not-always-so-healthy feeling of envy. A recipe for life, like a recipe for any other dish, consists of ingredients: we are privileged to take from other people's recipes for life all those ingredients that arouse our curiosity and sincere interest.

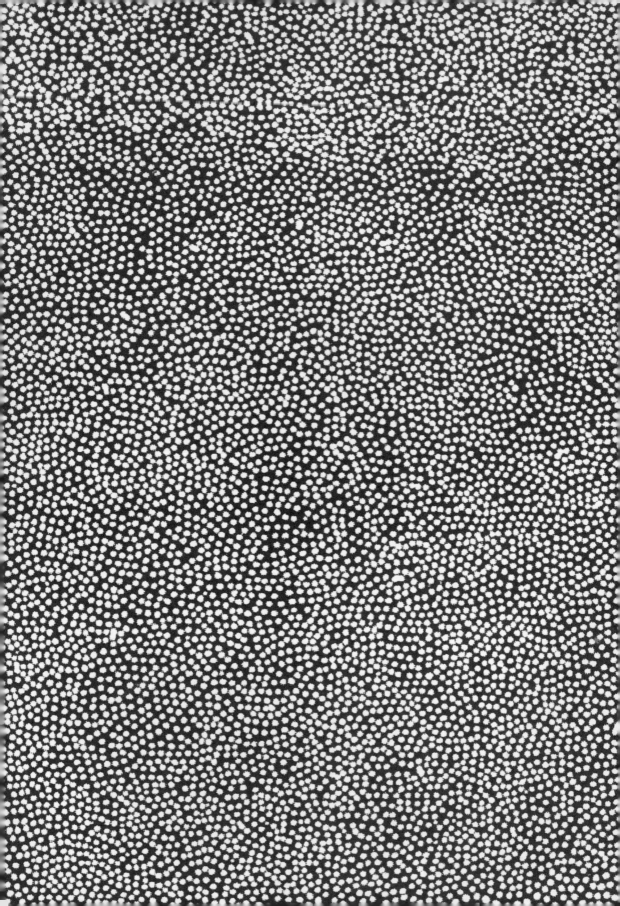

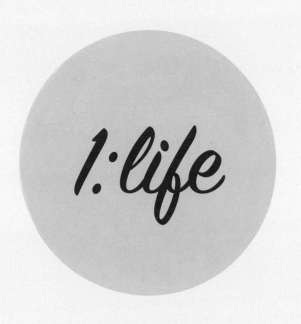

1: life

Who does not dream of another life? It's a tall order being someone else; what's it like? We need a few pointers, a few clues, some helpful examples. Here they are.

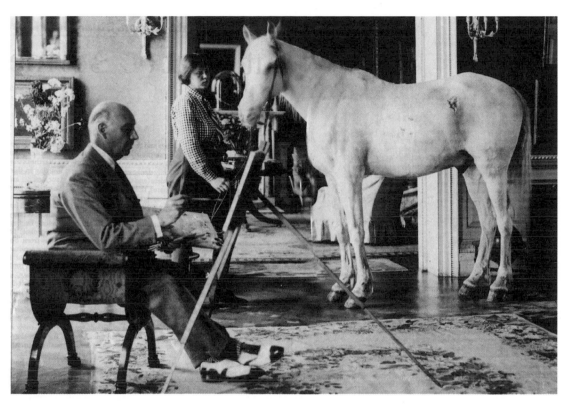

Lord Berners painting Penelope Betjeman and her pony at Faringdon in 1938

LIVE LIKE GERTRUDE STEIN

Miss Stein gets up every morning about ten and drinks some coffee, against her will. She's always been nervous about becoming nervous and she thought coffee would make her nervous, but her doctor prescribed it. Miss Toklas, her companion, gets up at six and starts dusting and fussing around... Every morning Miss Toklas bathes and combs their French poodle, Basket, and brushes its teeth. It has its own toothbrush.

Miss Stein has an outsize bathtub that was especially made for her. A staircase had to be taken out to install it. After her bath she puts on a huge wool bathrobe and writes for a while, but she prefers to write outdoors, after she gets dressed. Especially in the Ain country, because there are rocks and cows there. Miss Stein likes to look at rocks and cows in the intervals of her writing. The two ladies drive around in their Ford till they come to a good spot. Then Miss Stein gets out and sits on a campstool with pencil and pad, and Miss Toklas fearlessly switches a cow into her line of vision. If the cow doesn't seem to fit in with Miss Stein's mood, the ladies get into the car and drive on to another cow. When the great lady has an inspiration, she writes quickly, for about fifteen minutes. But often she just sits there, looking at cows and not turning a wheel.

Miss Stein always drives, and Miss Toklas rides in the back seat, squealing and jumping, for they say that Miss Stein is the worst driver in the history of automotive engineering. She takes corners fast, doesn't put out her hand, drives on the wrong side of the street, pays no more attention to traffic signals or intersections than she does to punctuation marks, and never honks. Now and then Alice will lean over from the back seat and honk...

Miss Stein spends much of her time quarrelling with friends — always about literature or painting. The quarrels are passionate ones, involving everybody, taking hours to get under way, lasting for years (like the one with Hemingway). Nobody remembers after a couple of months exactly what the quarrels are about. The maid at the Stein house in Paris has to be told every day who will be persona grata at tea — it all depends on the quarrel of the night before. Gertrude sits up late, talking, arguing, and laughing; she has a rich, deep, and warming laugh. Afterward she wakes up Alice, who goes to bed early, and they go over the talk of the whole day. Miss Stein has a photographic memory for conversation.

The lady wears astonishing clothes: sandals, woollen stockings fit for a football-player, a man's plush fedora hat perched high on her head, rough tweed suits over odd embroidered waistcoats and peasant tunics. She also wears extraordinary blue-and-white striped knickers for underdrawers. This came out when she lost them once at a concert given by Virgil Thomson at the Hotel Majestic. She just stepped out of them somehow and left them lying there on the floor. She thought it was very funny and laughed loudly.

Janet Flanner, James Thurber and Harold Ross, *New Yorker*, 13 October 1934

LIVE LIKE THE LAST OF THE MEDICI

Wake at midday as donkey enters bearing panniers of peaches, grapes and other fruit. Reach out languid hand. Lie in bed till dinner at five, when entourage of boys comes in to entertain you.

From Will Hobson, *The Household Box: New Ways To Enjoy Your Home, Relationships, Family and Life!*, 2011

LIVE LIKE PHILIP LARKIN

My life is as simple as I can make it. Work all day, cook, eat, wash up, telephone, hack writing, drink, television in the evenings. I almost never go out. I suppose everyone tries to ignore the passing of time — some people by doing a lot, being in California one year and Japan the next. Or there's my way — making every day and every year exactly the same. Probably neither works.

From *Paris Review*, 1982

DRINK LIKE HUNTER S. THOMPSON

3pm – Rise 3.05 – Chivas Regal with the morning papers, Dunhill cigarette 3.45 – cocaine 3.50 – another glass of Chivas, Dunhill 4.05 – first cup of coffee, Dunhill 4.15 – cocaine 4.16 – orange juice, Dunhill 4.30 cocaine 4.54 cocaine 5.05 – cocaine 5.11 – coffee, Dunhills 5.30 – more ice in the Chivas 5.45 – cocaine 6pm – grass to take the edge off 7.05 – Woody Creek Tavern for lunch – Heineken, two margaritas, two cheeseburgers, two orders of fries, a plate of tomatoes, coleslaw, a taco salad, a double order of onion rings, carrot cake, ice cream, bean fritter, Dunhills, another Heineken, cocaine, and for the ride home, a snow cone (a glass of shredded ice over which is poured three or four jiggers of Chivas) 5pm – cocaine 10pm – drops acid 11pm – Chartreuse, cocaine, grass Midnight – Hunter ready to write 12.05–6am – Chatreuse, cocaine, grass, Chivas, coffee, Heineken, clove cigarettes, grapefruit, Dunhills, orange juice, gin 6am – in the hot tub, champagne, Dove Bars, fettucine Alfredo 8am – Halcion 8.20 – sleep.

From E. Jean Carroll, *Hunter: The Strange and Savage Life of Hunter S. Thompson*, 1993

LIVE LIKE MAYA ANGELOU

When you are refreshed by the Bible and the sherry, how do you start a day's work?

I have kept a hotel room in every town I've ever lived in. I rent a hotel room for a few months, leave my home at six, and try to be at work by six-thirty. To write, I lie across the bed, so that this elbow is absolutely encrusted at the end, just so rough with callouses. I never allow the hotel people to change the bed, because I never sleep there. I stay until twelve-thirty or one-thirty in the afternoon, and then I go home and try to breathe; I look at the work around five; I have an orderly dinner – proper, quiet, lovely dinner; and then I go back to work the next morning. Sometimes in hotels I'll go into the room and there'll be a note on the floor which says, Dear Miss Angelou, let us change the sheets. We think they are moldy. But I only allow them to come in and empty wastebaskets. I insist that all things are taken off the walls. I don't want anything in there. I go into the room and I feel as if all my beliefs are suspended. Nothing holds me to anything. No milkmaids, no flowers, nothing. I just want to feel and then when I start to work I'll remember. I'll read something, maybe the Psalms, maybe, again, something from Mr. Dunbar, James Weldon Johnson. And I'll remember how beautiful, how pliable the language is, how it will lend itself.

From George Plimpton, *Paris Review*, issue 116, autumn 1990

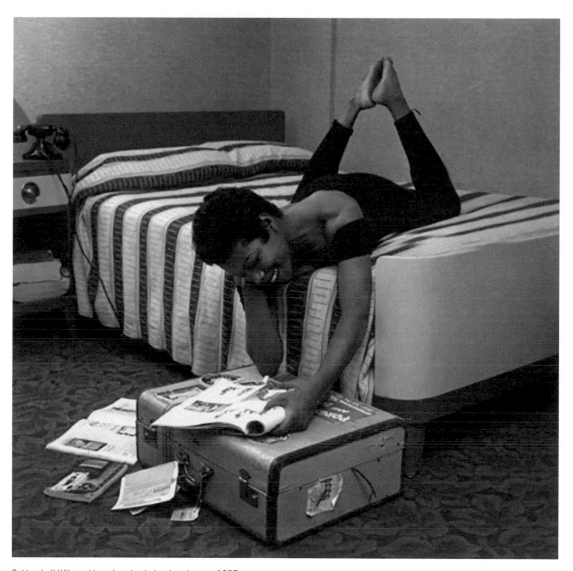

G. Marshall Wilson, Maya Angelou in her hotel room, 1957

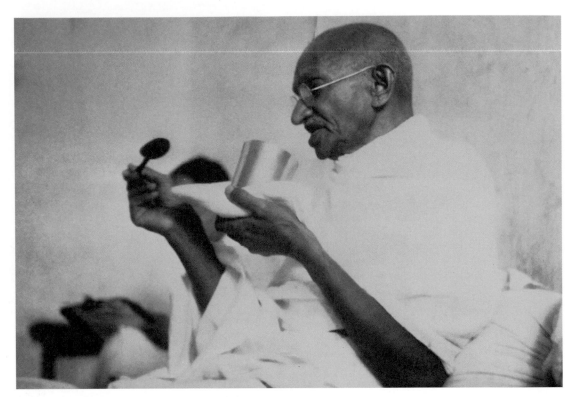

Ghandi eats a meal in preparation for a fast, March 1940

EAT LIKE MAHATMA GANDHI

The first entry of Gandhi's raw-food diary, dated 22 August 1893: 'Began the vital food experiment ... Had two tablespoonfuls of wheat, one of peas, one of rice, two of sultanas, about twenty small nuts, two oranges, and a cup of cocoa for breakfast.' He soaked the wheat, peas, and rice overnight, but did not cook them. He took 45 minutes to eat the meal, which left him feeling 'very bright in the morning'.

From Nico Slate, *Ghandhi's Search for the Perfect Diet*, 2019

LIVE LIKE MARK WAHLBERG

On a typical day, the actor rises at 02:30, before half an hour of prayers. After breakfast at 03:15, he does a 95-minute workout followed by another meal, shower, snack, golf and 'cryo chamber recovery' (a treatment favoured by athletes using liquid nitrogen to briefly plunge the air to temperature below −100°C to alleviate muscle and joint pain) – all before 10:30.

Wahlberg goes to bed at 7.30 pm with an hour and a half set aside for a shower, followed by half an hour devoted to playing golf.

And then there's the food intake.

'I start out with steel oats, blueberries and peanut butter for breakfast – then I have a protein shake, three turkey burgers, five pieces of sweet potato at about 5:30 in the morning. At 8 o'clock, I have about 10 turkey meatballs. At 10:30 am, I have a grilled chicken salad with two hard-boiled eggs, olives, avocado, cucumber, tomato, lettuce.

'Then at 1 o'clock I have a New York steak with green peppers. At 3.30 pm, I have grilled chicken with bok choi. At 5.30/6 o'clock, I have a beautiful piece of halibut or cod or a seabass, with some vegetables, maybe some sauté potatoes and bok choi. And I have a lot of Aquahydrate during the day. That's it.'

From BBC News, 2018

LIVE LIKE DJUNA BARNES

Djuna Barnes, according to one of her biographers, spent more than fifteen thousand days, that is, more than forty years, alone in her apartment in Patchin Place.

'And we know that most of them, days and years, passed in total silence without her exchanging a single word with anyone … In 1931, long before those forty years began, she had written: 'I like my human experience served up with a little silence and restraint. Silence makes experience go further, and when it does die, gives it that dignity common to a thing one had touched and not ravished.'

No one saw very much of her during this interminable old age. She was afraid of the adolescents who hung around in the streets. She had such a horror of beards that she even phoned a future visitor and demanded that he shave his off (she had enquired about his appearance) before he came to see her …

The few people who visited her before that date spent long hours with her and always ended up with a headache. 'I've been told that I give everyone I talk to a headache,' she said. The response of the afflicted visitor was: 'You're so intense!' And she said: 'Yes, I know.'

From Javier de Marías, *Written Lives*, 1992

LIVE LIKE A CHILD IN THE 1950s

Many many hours of my childhood were spent in learning how to whistle. In learning how to snap my fingers. In hanging from the branch of a tree. In looking in an ants' nest. In digging holes. Making piles. Tearing things down. Throwing rocks at things. ...

We strung beads on strings: we strung spools on strings; we tied each other up with string, and belts and clothesline.

We sat in boxes; we sat under porches; we sat on roofs; we sat on limbs of trees.

We stood on boards over excavations; we stood on top of piles of leaves; we stood under rain dripping from the eaves; we stood up to our ears in snow.

We looked at things like knives and immies and pig nuts and grasshoppers and clouds and dogs and people.

We skipped and hopped and jumped. Not going anywhere – just skipping and hopping and jumping and galloping.

We sang and whistled and hummed and screamed.

What I mean is, Jack, we did a lot of nothing.

From Robert Paul Smith, *Where Did You Go? Out. What Did You Do? Nothing*, 1957

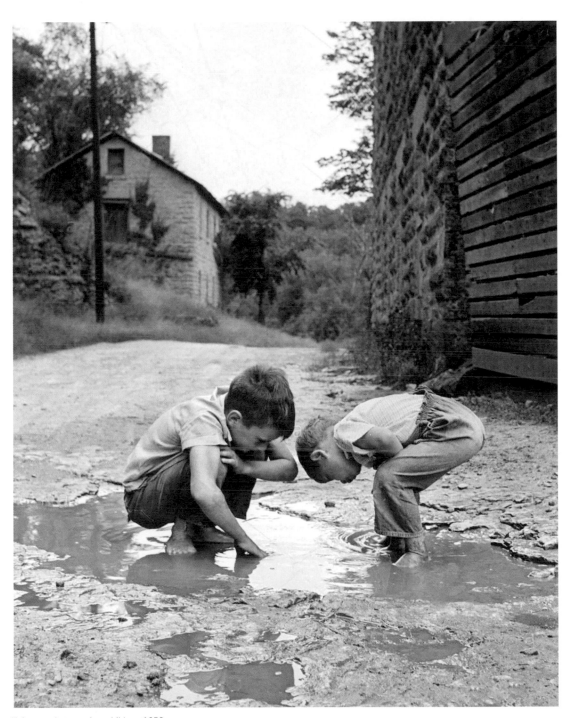

Unknown photographer, children, 1950s

LIVE LIKE ANTON CHEKHOV

I am of the opinion that real happiness is impossible without idleness. My ideal is to be idle and love a plump young girl. My most intense pleasure is to walk or sit doing nothing; my favourite occupation is picking useless stuff (leaves, straw, and so on) and doing useless things.

From a letter to Lydia Mizinova, 27 March 1894

EAT LIKE PATRICIA HIGHSMITH

Novelist Patricia Highsmith ate the same thing for virtually every meal: bacon and fried eggs. She began each writing session with a stiff drink – 'not to perk her up', according to her biographer, Andrew Wilson, 'but to reduce her energy levels, which veered towards the manic'. Then she would sit on her bed surrounded by cigarettes, coffee, a doughnut and a saucer of sugar, the intention being 'to avoid any sense of discipline and make the act of writing as pleasurable as possible'.

From Killian Fox, *The Gannet's Gastronomic Miscellany*, 2017

DON'T BEHAVE LIKE HENRY BRADSHAW

Henry Bradshaw, Librarian of Cambridge University from 1867–1886, had a number of blind spots. 'It has been my curse all through life that I want the power or gift, or whatever you like to call it, of finishing what I work at, and all the minute research in the world is only rendered more hopeless by this failing.' He was very 'variable about correspondence'. Sometimes he would write two or three times a week to friends, at others nothing would extract an answer from him. 'He was unable at times to return any answer to an invitation, and it is a well-known anecdote how a friend of his, who had invited him to dinner and could get no reply, sent him two postcards, addressed to himself, on one of which was "Yes," and on the other "No." Bradshaw posted them both.'

From Arthur C. Benson, *The Leaves of the Tree*, 1911

LIVE LIKE W. H. AUDEN

'Martini-time,' Auden wrote in a poem describing his view of life at Kirchstetten, 'time to draw the curtains and / choose a composer we should like to hear from.' The radiogram would be switched on and the records of Bellini or Donizetti or Richard Strauss played and argued over, while Auden supervised the mixing of what one guest described as 'the strongest martinis I ever drank'. There were strict rules for this: at mid-day the vodka and the glasses themselves were put into the refrigerator, the vermouth (Noilly Prat) being added at a ration of about one measure to three of vodka an hour before serving. (Auden had originally made his martinis with gin, but Chester found that vodka had a better effect on him and Auden eventually decided to switch to it.) The result was described by one of Auden's friends as 'lethal'.

Dinner would be accompanied by plenty of wine, usually a Valpolicella, and afterwards there would be more wine and records. Then, quite early, perhaps at half past nine, Auden would look at his watch and, abruptly announcing his bedtime, would disappear to his own room, where the bedclothes were piled so thickly on his bed that (as Michael Yates remarked) it looked like a blanket store. Here he would smoke a few more cigarettes and drink some wine while reading, before dropping off to sleep.

From Humphrey Carpenter, *W. H. Auden:* A Biography, 1981

LIVE LIKE MARCEL PROUST

All the hotel guests talked about how Monsieur Proust rented five expensive rooms, one to live in, the other four to 'contain' the silence.

Sometimes you found him seated at a big table. He would offer those who approached a glass of champagne. When he called for cigars for his friends, you knew he was about to leave.

'Excuse me,' he'd say. 'The cigar smoke makes me cough.'

And he would stand up. He seemed to be in a hurry to get back to his room and the silence.

Frrom Philippe Soupault, *Paris Review*, 2016, describing a stay at the Grand Hotel in Cabourg in 1913, where Proust spent his summers.

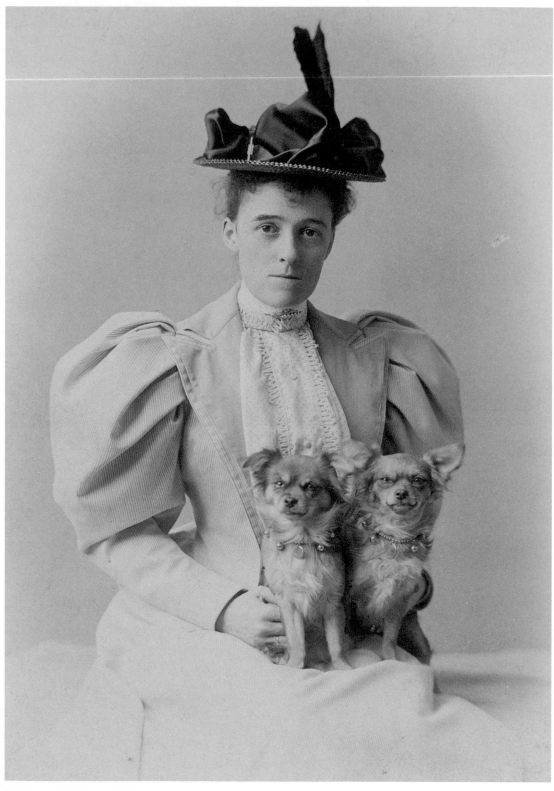

E. F. Cooper, *Edith Wharton*, 1895

BEHAVE LIKE EDITH WHARTON

[Henry James] almost never spoke about his own works, but lavished great care on his library, which he himself dusted with a silk handkerchief. He did not understand why his books did not sell better than they did, although *Daisy Miller* was very nearly a best-seller. His friend Edith Wharton once asked their joint publisher to pay her far larger royalties into James's account. James never found out.

From Javier de Marías, *Written Lives*, 1992

LIVE LIKE PETER THE GREAT

Up at six, chop wood with entire court until cannon sounds at eleven, lunch with vodka, sleep till four, paperwork, ambassadors till seven, party till one.

From Will Hobson, *The Household Box: New Ways To Enjoy Your Home, Relationships, Family and Life!*, 2011

EAT LIKE RAYMOND RADIGUET

On the opening night of Le Boeuf sur le Toit, a nightclub named after a musical entertainment written by Jean Cocteau with Erik Satie and Darius Milhaud, Cocteau, the star of the evening, lost sight of the writer Raymond Radiguet, with whom he was in love.

'Thirsty for more and stronger booze, and irritated with Cocteau's behaviour, Radiguet had made his way to the bar to join Constantin Brancusi, the Romanian sculptor. Brancusi was fed up too, so the two men went off with (the artist Nina) Hamnett to Montparnasse. After a bit of wandering, Brancusi proposed that they go to the Gare de Lyon to have a midnight bouillabaisse. They did so, but the dish was not to their taste, so the two men decided to go off in search of a better one – in Marseilles. Ditching Hamnett, they boarded the night train southwards. Alas, when they arrived in Marseilles, they found that the local version of the dish was not greatly to their taste either, so after a protracted bout of heavy drinking they got on a boat to Corsica. For about a week they stayed in a huge, freezing hotel, keeping themselves warm (or under the illusion that they were warm) by drinking gallons of Corsican brandy. They finally made it back to Paris, and the Boeuf, ten days later. Cocteau was furious; Brancusi never went back to the nightclub.'

From Kevin Jackson, *Constellation of Genius: 1922: Modernism And All That Jazz*, 2013

DON'T BEHAVE LIKE BHALO

[The *taarab* singer] Bhalo has a history of creating public discontent. He is known specifically for creating embarrassing situations. At a 1990 wedding in Lamu, for example, where he was invited to perform *taarab* at the reception held at the bride's home, Bhalo openly castigated the bride for being too fat. He sang one of his earlier compositions, 'Gunia' (Gunny Sack) in reference to the bride. In the song, Bhalo searches for someone to help him carry his very heavy sack, trying the makuli (dock workers, stevedores), *mijinunda* (strong and heavily built people), *hamali* (heavy load carriers), and a crane driver, but none could help him. While he did not mention the bride directly, my informants all agreed that anybody attending the wedding knew to whom Bhalo was referring. Indeed, he performed this song as the bride arrived.

From Gunderson and Barz, eds, Mwenda Ntarangwi, 'Malumbano and Matukano: Competition, Confrontation, and the (De)Construction of Masculinity in the Taarab of Maulidi and Bhalo', in *Mashindano!: Competitive Music Performance in East Africa*, 2000

BEHAVE LIKE JANE BOWLES

The poet Allen Ginsberg once rang Jane and Paul Bowles's house in Tangiers. Jane Bowles answered:
'Then this complete madman asked if I believed in God. "Do you believe in God, Jane?"
I told him: "I'm certainly not going to discuss it on the telephone."'

From Lorna Sage, introduction to Jane Bowles, *Two Serious Ladies*, 2018

LIVE LIKE AN ELEPHANT

Lie down for 2–4 hours sleep first thing, then start on day's 12–18 hours eating. Browse in the woodland, then emerge in the cool of the late afternoon to graze on grassland, or concentrate on succulent leaves and fruits in rainforest. Drink a lot, without sucking water all the way up trunk into nose (as if you need reminding). Strip bark from trees, get salt off rocks with tusks. Your four teeth – molars – could suffer the effects of eating up to 300 kg of abrasive food a day, and at times your 35 m long intestine will, literally, weigh a tonne. Stop for snooze in the shade. Go for a swim; paddle with all four feet; use trunk as a snorkel.

From Will Hobson, *The Household Box: New Ways To Enjoy Your Home, Relationships, Family and Life!*, 2011

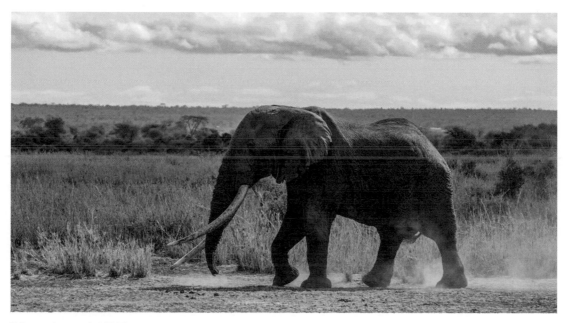

Unknown photographer, 2017

LIVE LIKE ERIK SATIE

An artist must organise his life. Here is the exact timetable of my daily activities:

I rise at 7:18 am inspired from 10:23 to 11:47. I lunch at 12:11 and leave the table at 12:14. A healthy ride on horseback round my domain follows from 1:19 pm to 2:53 pm. Another bout of inspiration from 3:12 to 4:07 pm From 4:27 to 6:47 pm various occupations (fencing, reflection, immobility, visits, contemplation, dexterity, swimming, etc.).

Dinner is served at 7:16 and finished at 7:20 pm. From 8:09 to 9:59 pm symphonic readings (out loud). I go to bed regularly at 10:37 pm Once a week, I wake up with a start at 3:19 (Tuesdays).

My only nourishment consists of food that is white: eggs, sugar, grated bones, the fat of dead animals, veal, salt, coconuts, chicken cooked in white water, fruit-mould, rice, turnips, camphorated sausages, pastry, cheese (white varieties), cotton salad and certain kinds of fish (without their skin). I boil my wine and drink it cold mixed with the juice of the fuchsia. I am a hearty eater, but never speak while eating, for fear of strangling.

I breathe with care (a little at a time). I very rarely dance. When walking, I clasp my sides, and look steadily behind me.

My expression is very serious; when I laugh it is unintentional, and I always apologise most affably.

I sleep with only one eye closed, very profoundly. My bed is round, with a hole to put my head through. Once every hour a servant takes my temperature and gives me another.

I have subscribed for some time to a fashion magazine. I wear a white cap, white stockings and a white waistcoat.

My doctor has always told me to smoke. Part of his advice runs: 'Smoke away, dear chap; if you don't someone else will.'

From Erik Satie's *Memoirs of an Amnesiac, To Be Read Far from the Herd and the Mummified Dead, Those Great Scourges of Humanity*, 1912

EAT LIKE SOPHIE CALLE

In a 1997 photo series called 'The Chromatic Diet', the French artist Sophie Calle set out to create a meal each day only using ingredients of the same colour. The project is a direct response to author Paul Auster's *Leviathan*, in which the protagonist (based on Calle) performs this very eating ritual.

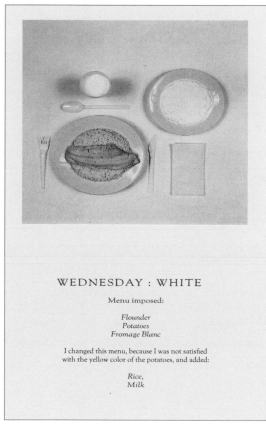

WEDNESDAY : WHITE

Menu imposed:

Flounder
Potatoes
Fromage Blanc

I changed this menu, because I was not satisfied
with the yellow color of the potatoes, and added:

Rice,
Milk

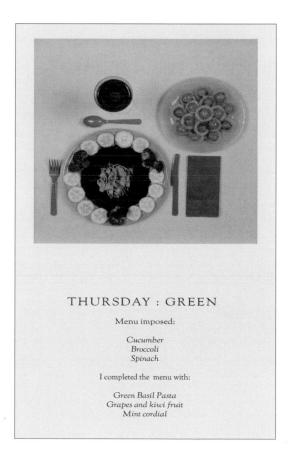

THURSDAY : GREEN

Menu imposed:

Cucumber
Broccoli
Spinach

I completed the menu with:

Green Basil Pasta
Grapes and kiwi fruit
Mint cordial

From Sophie Calle, *Le Régime Chromatique*, 1997

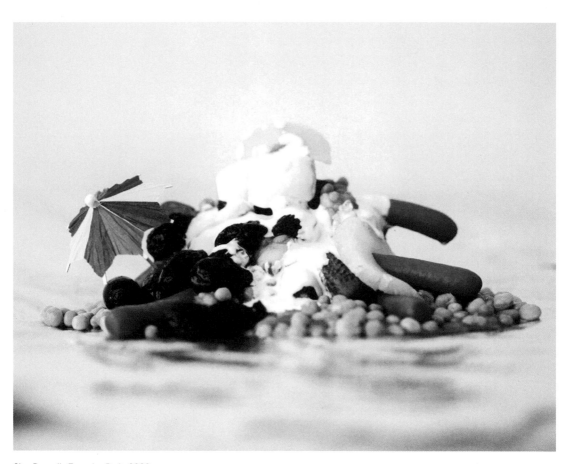

Sian Bonnell, *Everyday Dada*, 2006

COOK LIKE STEFAN HAUS

INGREDIENTS:

1 birth certificate 1 family album 1 history book   1 cup of all-purpose flour   1 teaspoon salt   2 cups of milk
1 cup of mineral water   2 tablespoons of olive oil   1 large egg   Assorted toppings, such as Nutella, parsley, honey, jams, sweetened whipped cream, or chocolate syrup.

INSTRUCTIONS:

1. Use the scissors and slice up your birth certificate, all the photos from your family album and all the pages from the history book.
2. Whisk the whole egg, mix until you get a thick homogeneous mixture, pour the milk and mix.
3. Then, stirring constantly with a whisk, pour in the flour until you have used up the given measure, add a pinch of salt.
4. If the mixture seems thick, dilute it with mineral water. Add the bits and pieces of paper and photographs you have sliced.
5. Set a medium frying pan or crêpe pan over a medium heat and carefully wipe it with some oiled kitchen paper.
6. When hot, cook your pancakes for 1 min. on each side until golden, keeping them warm in a low oven as you go.

Remember not to cry your tears onto the pan and the pancakes because you're sad over the family photos. The tears are salty and they can ruin the whole thing. You can spread the pancakes with Nutella, jam, honey or whatever else will make your rebirth tasty. Once you have eaten the evidence of your birth and family connections, you will start anew. It's best to make it as sweet as possible.

From Stefan Haus, *Happy Birthday*, 2020

COOK LIKE THE CEDILLA

CEDILLIC:

    6 pounds of zebra

    18 pounds of dolphin

    4 pounds of lynx

    9 tame dormice

    2 owls

    5 litres of whale oil

    dandelion root

    willow leaves

HERBS

    garam masala

    powdered fresh coffee

    palm tree kernels

    cactus hearts

    ocean water

    river water

Put the ocean water in a large cauldron over the fire. Disembowel and clean the animals, whose variety must be as great as possible, and who give their best flavour when they have just been caught, and not waiting in captivity. Clean the dandelion root and the willow leaves. Throw into the boiling water the animals cut into small pieces, add the whale oil, dandelion root and willow leaves, the garam masala, powdered coffee, palm tree kernels and cactus hearts. Let simmer on a slow fire for several days, adding river water if necessary. Pour the bouillon on tortillas and serve the meat in a hollow plate, or serve them both together. It is possible to make the dish even more tasty by adding, first, one little pickle cut in slices; second, geranium petals (vigorously wash them before parting them). They will be added to the dish two seconds before serving.

SERVES: 2 Vostells / 39 Brechts / 1000 Maciunases / 8 Dick Higginses / 1 Emmett Williams

From George Brecht and Robert Filiou, *Games at the Cedilla*, a compendium of correspondence, ideas, notations, journal records and games, 1967

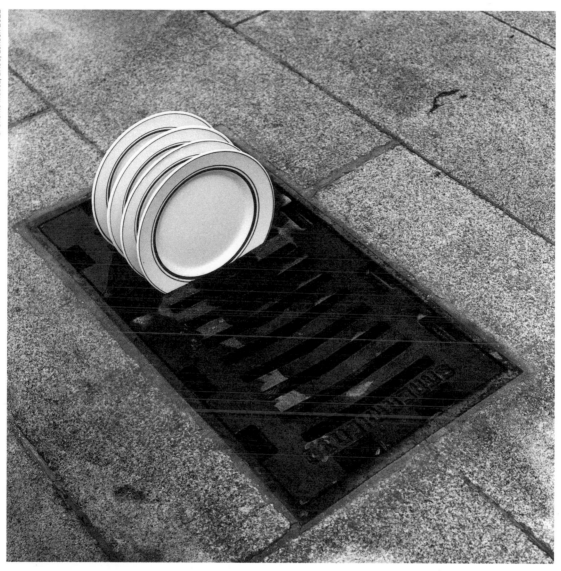

Chema Madoz, *Untitled*, 1998

COOK LIKE LOUISE BOURGEOIS

I love to cook. It amuses and relaxes me but when it comes time to serve the food, I lose confidence in myself. once made *boeuf à la mode* and spent all afternoon preparing it. When it was time to eat none of my family would come to the table. I was angry at first, then hurt, so I took the *boeuf à la mode* and threw it out the window. Just at that precise moment the children came in the door. They did not understand that waiting for them to like my food was agony for me. They were so surprised.

From Nancy Kirk and Madeleine Conway, *The Museum of Modern Art Artists Cookbook: 155 Recipes: Conversations with Thirty Contemporary Painters and Sculptors*, 1977

EAT LIKE TERRY FROST

8 large black olives, stoned
Sea salt
Charcoal grill the olives on a skewer until spitting hot. Remove from the grill and sprinkle liberally with salt.
Place 3, 5 or 8 hot olives in the mouth. The resulting explosion clears the head.
Follow this with a glass of ouzo and continue your journey to Aphrodite with clarity.

From *The Artists' Cookbook*, 1957

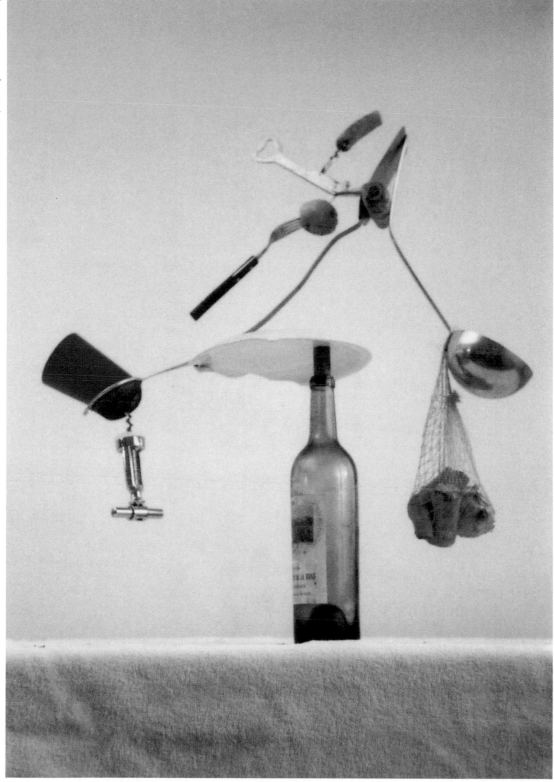

Peter Fischli and David Weiss, *The First Blush of Morning*, 1984

EVERYDAY BREAKFASTS

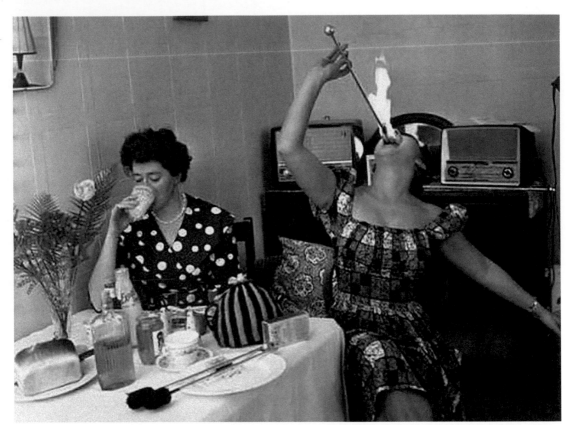

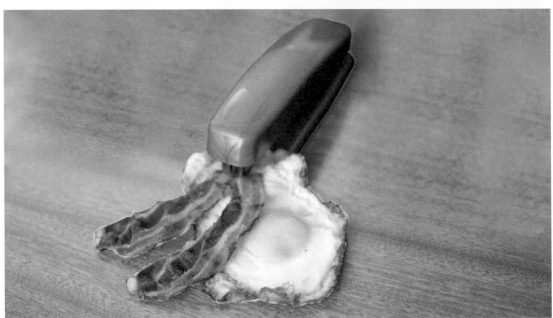

TOP: Unknown photographer   ABOVE: Sian Bonnell, *Everyday Dada*, 2006

ROOM SERVICE
BREAKFAST

To be served at:

☐ 7.00/7.30   ☐ 7.30/8.00   ☐ 8.00/8.30   ☐ 8.30/9.00   ☐ 9.00/9.30   ☐ 9.30/10.00   ☐ 10.00/10.30

Breakfast forms are picked up by 5.00am For any further request, please contact ....

Please mark your choice and number of orders desired in the appropriate box

☐ **Continental breakfast** with choice of rolls, croissant, brioches, rusks, bagels, various jams, honey, butter. **To drink:** ☐ Espresso ☐ Cappuccino ☐ Café au lait ☐ American coffee ☐ Sanka decaffeinated coffee Tea: ☐ Earl Grey ☐ Assam ☐ Darjeeling ☐ Lapsang Souchong ☐ Chai ☐ Green Tea ☐ Touareg Tea ☐ White Tea ☐ Iron Goddess of Mercy Tea ☐ Formosa Oolong ☐ milk ☐ lemon ☐ Ginger ☐ Hot chocolate ☐ *con churros* ☐ Hot milk ☐ Cold milk **Juices:** ☐ orange ☐ grapefruit ☐ tomato ☐ pineapple ☐ mango ☐ apple ☐ kiwi ☐ bitter gourd ☐ watermelon ☐ carrot ☐ honeydew melon ☐ pear ☐ banana ☐ papaya **Fruit, cereals, yoghurt:** ☐ Stewed fruit ☐ Corn flakes (Fiocchi di mais) ☐ Rice Krispies (Riso soffiato) ☐ Muesli (Müsli) ☐ Apple Zings ☐ Baron von Redberry ☐ C-3PO's ☐ Dudley Do-Right ☐ E.T. Cereal ☐ Frosted Mini-Spooners ☐ Golden Crisp ☐ Honey Bunches of Oats ☐ Just Right ☐ Kaboom! ☐ Life ☐ Morning Funnies ☐ Nut 'n Honey ☐ Oks ☐ Puffkins ☐ Quake ☐ Reptar Crunch ☐ Sir Grapefellow ☐ Triples ☐ Ultima Organic ☐ Vanilly Crunch ☐ Wheaties ☐ Plain yogurt ☐ **Fresh Country Eggs**, either: ☐ Fried (Al piatto) ☐ Scrambled (Uova strapazzate) ☐ Soft boiled (Alla coque) (minutes.......) ☐ Omelette: ☐ plain ☐ w/ cheese ☐ w/ ham

Any of the egg dishes can be served with bacon, fried/grilled tomatoes, mushrooms, fried bread, black pudding, grits, hash browns, biscuits, toast, pancakes, waffles, baked beans, kidneys, sausages or onions. Or with one of the other breakfasts. Kippers, kedgeree and corned beef available at weekends.

☐ **Afghani breakfast:** *koft'a*, meat, or *sabzi*, vegetable, with rice, cake, buttered toast, *Qaimaaq chai*, green tea with milk and rose essence or cardamom seeds.

☐ **Bangladeshi breakfast:** a selection of rotis and chapatis, chicken curry, *Nihari* mutton shank curry, daal.

☐ **Brazilian breakfast:** *misto-quente*, grilled ham and cheese sandwiches, a selection of corn orange and carrot cakes.

☐ **Burmese breakfast:** *mohinga*, rice noodles in fish soup, *htamin kyaw*, fried rice with boiled peas, *kao hnyin*, steamed rice wrapped in banana leaf served with a sprinkle of toasted snakefish flakes and green and red chili paste.

☐ **Cambodian breakfast:** choice of congees – rice, chicken, pig's blood or seafood – with salted eggs, pickled vegetables and dried fish.

☐ **Chinese breakfast:** stuffed rice rolls, fried bean curd and cellophane noodles soup, plain rice porridge with salted duck eggs, pickled vegetables, thousand-year eggs, soya milk.

☐ **Colombian breakfast:** *changua* - milk, scallions, and cheese soup.

☐ **Costa Rican breakfast:** Gallo Pinto, black beans and rice, *natilla*, sour cream, *Salsa Lizano* and corn tortilla.

☐ **Danish breakfast:** *rundstykker* (bread rolls), cheeses, jams, *wienerbrød*, pastries, schnapps.

☐ **Dominican Republic breakfast,** *mangu*, boiled plantains, with salami and fried cheese.

☐ **Dutch breakfast:** sliced bread with cheeses, cured meats, jams, *hagelslag*, chocolate sprinkles, apple syrup, and a selection of *ontbijtkoek*, including *Oudewijvenkoek*, 'old hags' cake,' with aniseed.

☐ **Egyptian breakfast:** *ful medames*, fava beans, *ta'amiya*, falafel, tomatoes, cucumbers, onions, pickled vegetables, cheeses.

☐ **Ghanaian breakfast:** Tom Brown (roasted maize flour) porridge, *waakye*, rice and beans in a spicy pawn and tomato sauce.

☐ **Gujarati breakfast:** a selection of *haandvo* and *dhokla*, savoury cakes with chickpeas and lentils, *theplas*, spiced parathas made with curds, masala puris with pickles and yogurt.

☐ **Hong Kong breakfast:** fried eggs sunny-side up with 3 green peas on the side, clear soup with macaroni and shredded ham, bread roll.

☐ **Indonesian breakfast:** *lontong sayur*, compressed rice and vegetables in a spicy curry sauce, jackfruit, noodles, deep fried redskin peanuts, *kerupuk*, prawn crackers.

☐ **Japanese breakfast:** fermented soybeans, miso soup, rice with *nori*, rice porridge, grilled fish, raw egg and pickled vegetables.

☐ **Korean breakfast:** kimchi, rice, radish, onion, seaweed, green onion, cucumber and squash soup (in a dried pollack stock).

☐ **Lebanese breakfast:** *labneh* (yoghurt), pita, cucumbers, tomatoes, onions, fresh mint, olive oil, *manakish*: ☐ thyme ☐ cheese ☐ meat

☐ **Malaysian and Singaporean breakfast:** *nasi lemak, roti prata*, kaya toast, half boiled eggs and wonton noodles, glutinous rice, bean curd, red bean soup.

☐ **Pakistani breakfast:** semolina *halva, aloo cholay*, spicy chickpea-and-potato curry, *puri*.

☐ **Polish breakfast:** *twarozek*, curd cheese with herbs, sandwiches, milk soup.

☐ **Southwestern Nigerian breakfast:** *gari* cereal (made from *cassava*) with sugar.

☐ **Sri Lankan breakfast:** fresh roti, *pittu*, string hoppers, milk rice, *appa*, coconut *sambol*, seeni-onion fried with chili and sugar *jaggery*, plantains, curry: ☐ fish ☐ meat ☐ vegetable

☐ **Swedish breakfast:** soft and crisp breads, cold cuts, caviar, cheeses, whole-grain porridge with milk and lingonberry jam, pâté with pickled cucumber, *blåbärssoppa*, blueberry-soup.

☐ **Thai breakfast:** *jok* (rice porridge), boiled rice with fish, pickles and dried shredded pork.

☐ **Turkish breakfast:** white sourdough bread, cheeses, jams – watermelon, walnut, plum, melon - tomatoes, cucumbers, olives, butter, honey, *kaymak*, clotted water buffalo cream.

☐ **Ugandan breakfast:** boiled cassava, *katogo*, green cooking bananas, in either a ☐ beef stew ☐ or vegetable sauce

☐ **Yoruban breakfast:** *Ógi* porridge with evaporated milk, *Acarajé*, ground bean paste fried in oil, *Moi moi*, ground bean paste wrapped in leaves and steamed.

Please note, a second (Bavarian, Polish and Austrian) breakfast is available at 10.30 a.m. with Weißwurst. Other breakfasts available on request.

From Will Hobson, *The Household Box: New Ways To Enjoy Your Home, Relationships, Family and Life!*, 2011

BECOME AN AESTHETE

Poetic Subjects

The capital city. Arrowroot. Water-bur. Colts. Hail. Bamboo grass. The round-leaved violet. Club moss. Water oats. Flat river-boats. The mandarin duck. The scattered chigaya reed. Lawns. The green vine. The pear tree. The jujube tree. The Althea.

Things That Lose By Being Painted

Pinks, cherry blossoms, yellow roses. Men or women who are praised as being beautiful.

Things That Gain By Being Painted

Pines. Autumn fields. Mountain villages and paths. Cranes and deer. A very cold winter scene; an unspeakably hot summer scene.

Things That Should Be Large

Priests. Fruit. Houses. Provision bags. Inksticks for inkstones.
Men's eyes: when they are too narrow, they look feminine. On the other hand, if they were as large as metal bowls, I should find them rather frightening.
Round braziers. Winter cherries. Pine trees. The petals of yellow roses.
Horse as well as oxen should be large.

Things That Make One's Heart Beat Faster

Sparrows feeding their young. To pass a place where babies are playing. To sleep in a room where some fine incense has been burnt. To notice that one's elegant Chinese mirror has become a little cloudy. To see a gentleman stop his carriage before one's gate and instruct his attendants to announce his arrival. To wash one's hair, make one's toilet, and put on a scented robe; even if not a soul sees one, these preparations still produce an inner pleasure.
It is night and one is expecting a visitor. Suddenly one is startled by the sound of rain-drops, which the wind blows against the shutters.

Things That Arouse A Fond Memory Of The Past

Dried hollyhock. The objects used during the display of dolls. To find a piece of deep violet or grape-coloured material that has been pressed between the pages of a notebook.
It is a rainy day and one is feeling bored. To pass the time, one starts looking through some old papers. And then one comes across the letters of a man one used to love.
Last year's paper fan. A night with a clear moon.

Things That Fall From The Sky

Snow. Hail. I do not like sleet, but when it is mixed with pure white snow it is very pretty.
Snow looks wonderful when it has fallen on a roof of cypress bark.
When snow begins to melt a little, or when only a small amount has fallen, it enters into all the cracks between the bricks, so that the roof is black in some places, pure white in others – most attractive.
I like drizzle and hail when they come down on a shingle roof. I also like frost on a shingle roof or in a garden.

From *The Pillow Book of Sei Shōnagon*, account of Japanese court life at the end of the 10th century AD by a lady-in-waiting to Empress Sadko. Translated by Ivan Morris.

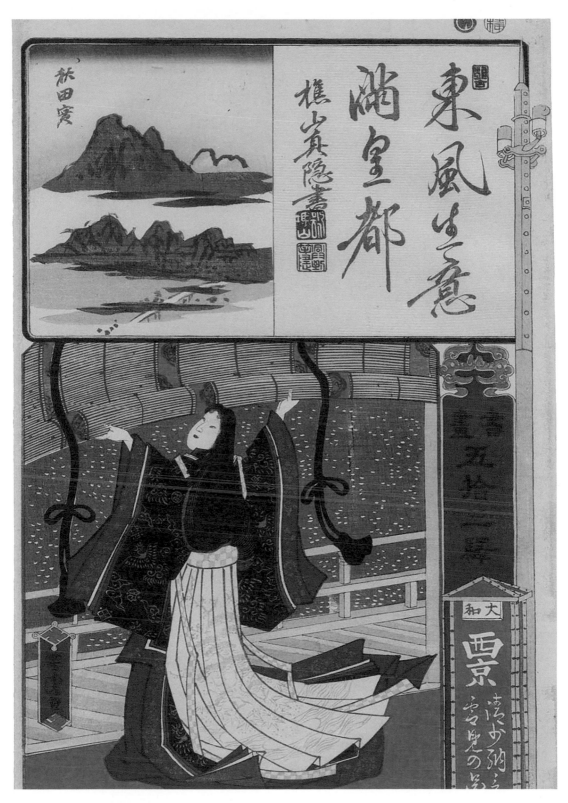

Utagawa Yoshitora, *Sei Shōnagon Viewing the Snow*, 1872

BECOME A BUDDHIST

WILL HOBSON

One thing all Buddhists share is the desire, at certain times, to go into retreat to devote themselves exclusively to spiritual study. A striking example of a retreat is the one performed by Diane Perry, originally from London's East End, who in 1976 secluded herself in a remote cave in the Himalayas, 13,200 feet above sea level. Known at this point by her Tibetan name, Tenzin Palmo, she spent the next twelve years in her cave, or 'cell for solitary confinement', as she called it, engaged in intense meditation. Her experiences are described in *Cave in The Snow* (1998).

Taking this as model, your cave should ideally be camouflaged, so no one can find you, and completely isolated. For a complete transformation, slap mud and cow dung on your home's floor and walls. Otherwise cover everything in sheets. Open all the windows. Despite being south-facing, your cave will get very cold, and you may get snowed in, a sensation akin to being buried alive. The only source of heat will be a small wood-burning stove, which you will use once a day to cook. Partition off a small area as a storeroom for food, thereby reducing your living space to 6 feet by 6 feet. A natural depression may serve as a bookshelf, but otherwise, apart from the stove, your furniture will consist of a wooden box for a table covered with a flowery tablecloth; a bucket, which will serve as your bath; an altar against the back wall, holding images of deities offering seven bowls full of water (the seven gifts), and, finally, a traditional meditation box, a square wooden structure measuring 2.6 feet by 2.6 feet, raised slightly off ground. Most of your days and all of your nights will be spent sitting upright in your meditation box. At no point should you lie down.

Your routine will revolve around four three-hour spells of meditation, from 3 am – 6 am, 8 am – 11 am, 3 pm – 6 pm, and 7 pm – 10 pm. Use your bucket to collect water from the spring, grow turnips and potatoes (the only vegetables that will survive the mice, hamsters, etc.), bake sourdough bread and make *tsampa* (barley porridge). Eat once a day, at midday. Stick to rice, dhal (lentils) and vegetables, brewed in a pressure cooker, which will count as your one luxury. Drink tea with powdered milk; have a small piece of fruit for dessert. In summer the outdoors will be your toilet; in winter, use a tin, and then bury it. Don't cut your hair. Eat flowers to feed your soul. Apart from the obvious physical privations, be prepared for a range of hardships, from flooding in spring to eye infections lasting months. Wild animals may visit, and you may have to steel yourself to walk through a colony of vultures. As a meditation practice, try *tonglen* ('giving and taking' in Tibetan) meditation. Visualise taking the suffering of others onto yourself on the in-breath, and on the out-breath giving happiness and success to all sentient beings. The aim is to reduce selfish attachment, increase a sense of renunciation, create positive karma by giving and helping, and develop loving kindness and *bodhicitta* (the wish to attain complete enlightenment).

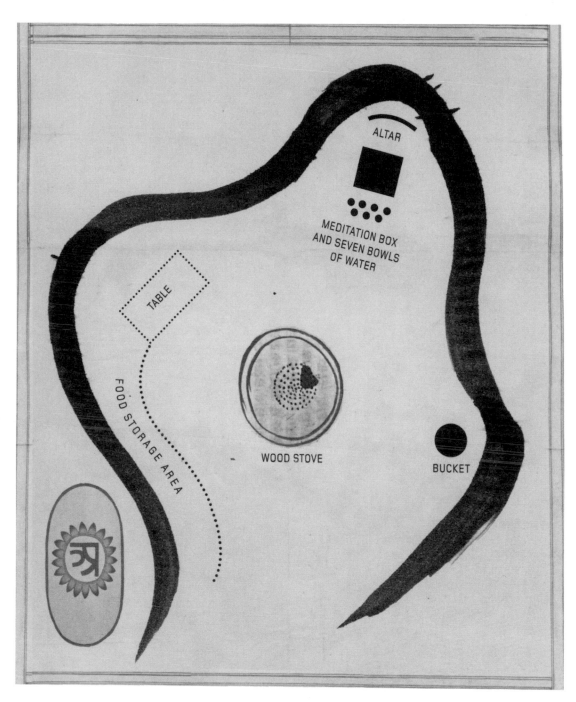

ALTAR

MEDITATION BOX
AND SEVEN BOWLS
OF WATER

TABLE

FOOD STORAGE AREA

WOOD STOVE

BUCKET

From Will Hobson, *The Household Box: New Ways To Enjoy Your Home, Relationships, Family and Life!*, 2011

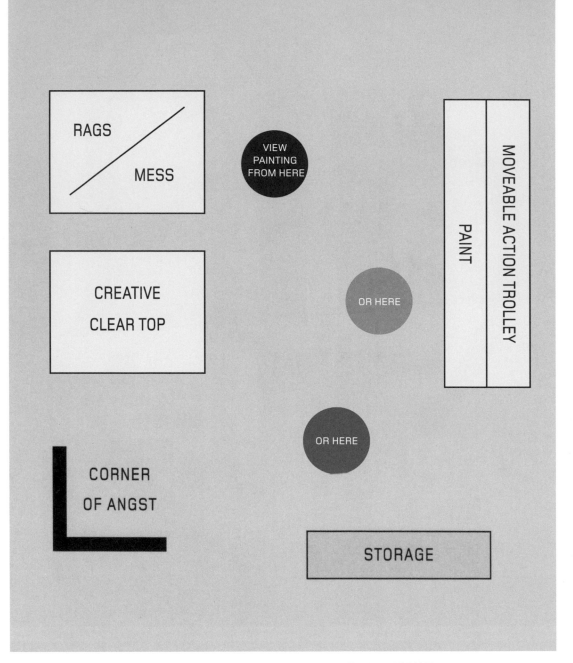

WALL OF ACTION

RAGS

MESS

VIEW PAINTING FROM HERE

CREATIVE CLEAR TOP

OR HERE

PAINT

MOVEABLE ACTION TROLLEY

OR HERE

CORNER OF ANGST

STORAGE

From Will Hobson, *The Household Box: New Ways To Enjoy Your Home, Relationships, Family and Life!*, 2011

BECOME AN ARTIST

WILL HOBSON

'Hello? Hello. Yes, I'm in the studio.' It's difficult to generalise about what artists need to make art, apart from desire and ambition. They think about what they do in such a variety of ways: Sarah Lucas, for instance, talks about making things to keep herself company, something she's done since she was a child; Mark Wallinger describes his favourite artists, Velázquez, Manet and Warhol, as holding up a radical mirror to society without succumbing to pedantry; Hedda Sterne used to refer to a need to understand and explain things to herself. As a consequence, their techniques and materials are extremely diverse; one constant, however, is the studio. This is where artists spend most of their days, generally alone. Everything else – galleries, an audience, the art world – flows from what goes on, or does not go on, in the studio.

So your studio may differ in its arrangement and contents from the painter's studio illustrated here but this will only be a technicality. The main thing is that this is where you'll spend your days come rain or shine – other commitments, jobs, people, etc. permitting. Your studio is the place where it will all happen – 'all' being the operative word. Much of your time in the studio will be spent trying out ideas and techniques, seeing what works. In fact, traditionally, 75 per cent of an artist's time is spent standing back and surveying what he or she has done, so you will need to choose a good position from which to do that. These represent possible vantage points in your studio for you to look at what you're working on. At times you'll be caught up in a blur of activity, at others the opposite.

At times you'll have eureka moments and feel a deep sense of achievement. At others, you'll feel the bitterest frustration at the chasm between what you want to do and what you are doing. At times you'll create and play to your heart's content, at others you'll suffer the most horrific doubts. In your mind you'll often have a dial like this:

The arrow will swing constantly, like a pendulum, between 'Genius' and 'Laughing Stock'. On occasion you'll feel a great sense of peace, as if you've transcended ego, and everything will flow calmly. Or you'll be struck by how things go in phases. Here you are, in your studio, and you're not feeling what you've felt for months. You're feeling something different now. And then the moment will come when you want to show other people your work.

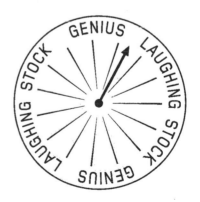

Will we admire you for having made it and wanting to show it to us? Yes.
Will that stop us disliking it? No.
Will some people wound you to the core with their criticisms? Yes.
Will that make you think of giving up? Maybe.
Will you give up? We hope not.

As Douglas Gordon said when he was asked what advice he'd give to young artists, 'Don't stop, don't stop, don't stop.'

BECOME KARL LAGERFELD

SIAN BONNNELL

This is all you'll need:

White card
Scissors
Black fingerless gloves
Some sort of bling on a chain
Large-sized dark glasses
Black jumper or jacket
Cat

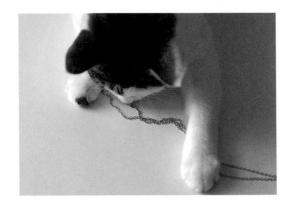

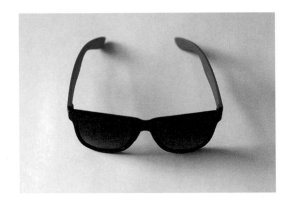

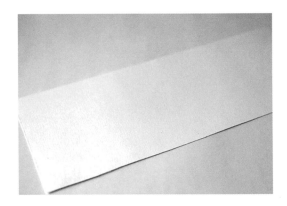

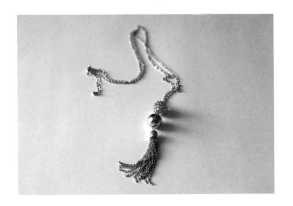

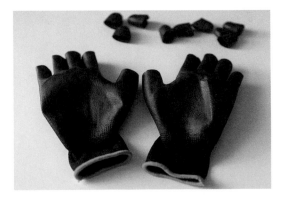

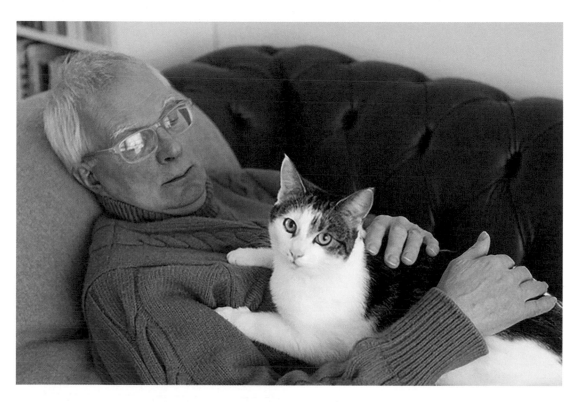

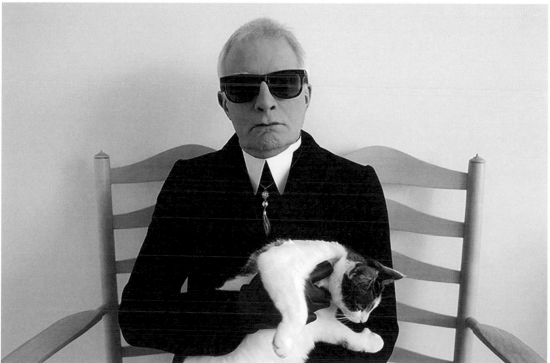

EMBRACE CHANGE

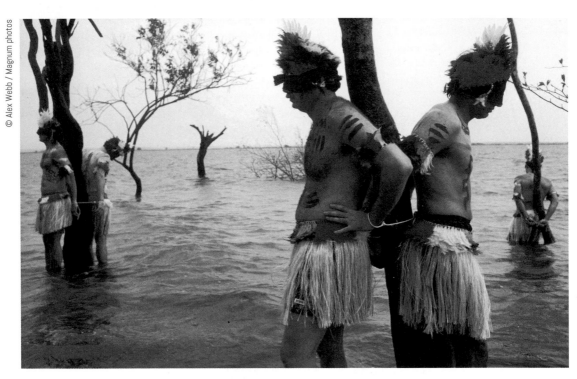

Alex Webb, North American real estate salesmen undergoing mock initiation ceremony, Manaus, Brazil, 1993

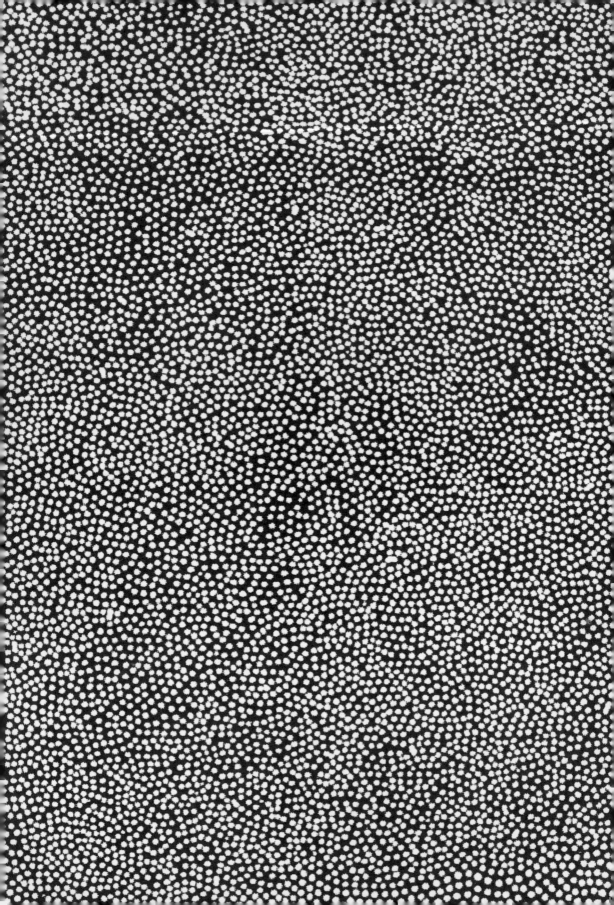

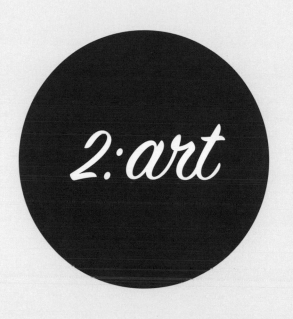

2:art

All serious art is the human imagination at play, and always has been; it constitutes human *being* at its most carefree even though artists call what they do 'work' or 'practice'. Sometime in the deep past it was realised that imaginative play was indeed work, that the mind should have parity of regard with the body, that everything wonderful in human life emerges from work of one kind or another.

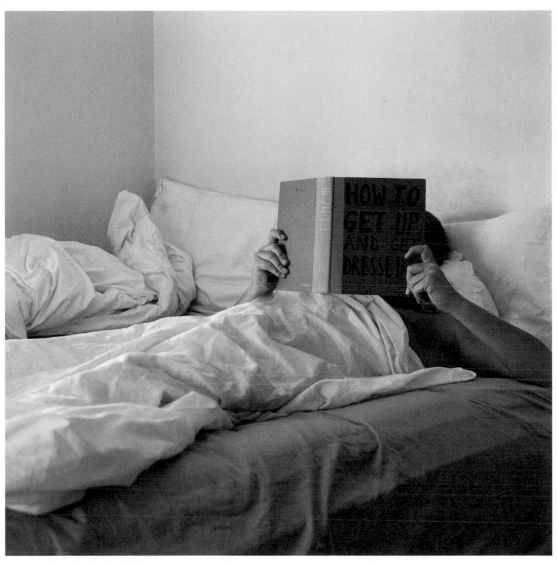

Friedrich Kunath, *Untitled*, 2009

LETTER WRITING

The artist Martin John Callanan created a book with a selection of responses to a series of letters mailed between 2004 and 2006, ranging from the bemused response of the Secretary to the Archbishop of Canterbury to the question *When will it end?* to appreciative letters from the offices of President Mubarak of Egypt in response to the declaration *I respect your authority*. Each letter poses a deceptively simple question or an inane rhetorical statement.

بسم الله الرحمن الرحيم

Public Relations

العلاقات العامة

                                        Cairo   2006

      Dear Mr. Martin John Callanan

            The Kind message of goodwill which you

      were good enought to send has been received

      with profound appreciation. his Excellency

      president Mubarak wishes to thank you and

      commends the spirit inspiring your noble

      sentiments .

                        Sincerely Yours.

                        Aly Ezzat

                        Head,

                        Central Department

                        of public Relation

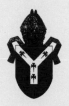

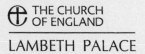

LAMBETH PALACE

Mr M Callanan
2 Arcadia Court
45 Old Castle Street
London
E1 7NY

Mr Andrew Nunn
Premises and Administration Secretary to
The Archbishop of Canterbury

25 April, 2006

Dear Mr Callanan

When will what end?

Yours sincerely

Andrew C

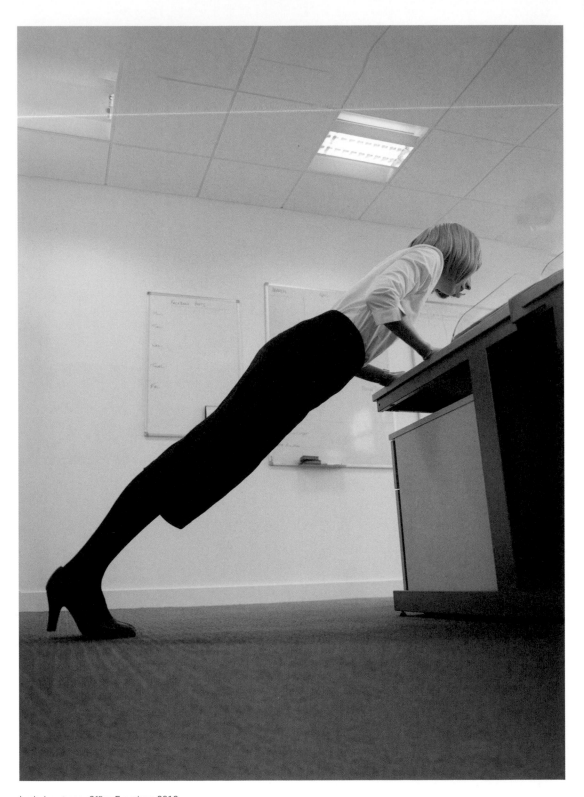

Lucie Armstrong, *Office Exercises*, 2019

Dear.............

Thank you for your letter rejecting my application for
employment with your firm.

I have received rejections from an unusually large number of
well qualified organisations. With such a varied and promising
spectrum of rejections from which to select, it is impossible
for me to consider them all. After careful deliberation, then,
and because a number of firms have found me more unsuitable,
I regret to inform you that I am unable to accept your
rejection.

Despite your company's outstanding qualifications and previous
experience in rejecting applicants, I find that your rejection
does not meet with my requirements at this time. As a result,
I will be starting employment with your firm on the first of
the month.

Circumstances change and one can never know when new demands
for rejection arise. Accordingly I will keep your letter on
file in case my requirements for rejection change.

Please do not regard this letter as a criticism of your
qualifications in attempting to refuse me employment.

I wish you the best of luck in rejecting future candidates.

Sincerely,

John Kador

John Kador, *Rejection Letter*, 2000

A Pablo Picasso Event
(in the form of telegrams)

```
DEAR PABLO
WE ARE THINKING OF PUTTING OUT PABLO PICASSO NECKTIES IN AN EDITION OF
30,000 EACH WITH A DIFFERENT REPRODUCTION ON ONE OF YOUR PAINTINGS   OK

LA CEDILLE QUI SOURIT
```

```
DEAR CEDILLE
ARE YOU OUT OF YOUR MIND
PABLO
```

```
DEAR ROY LICHTENSTEIN
```

From George Brecht and Robert Filiou, *Games at the Cedilla*, a compendium of correspondence, notations, journal records and games, 1967

FOUND OBJECTS

All sorts of different objects can be transformed into something unexpected and strange. The African artist Romuald Hazoumè often makes mask-like sculptures using discarded plastic gasoline canisters.

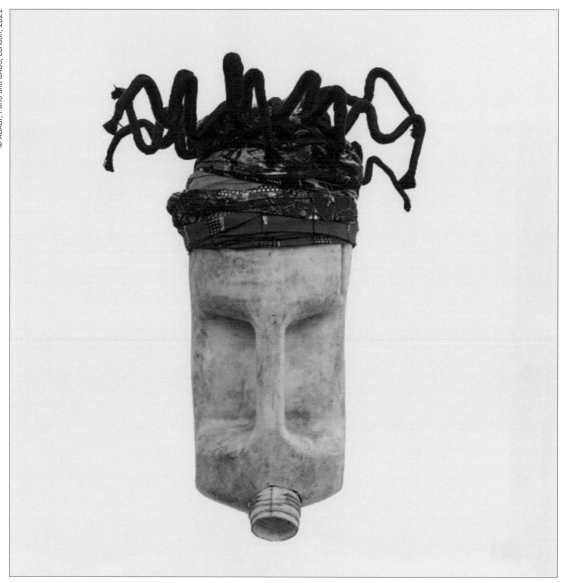

Romuald Hazoumè, *Azonto,* 2016

ONE MINUTE SCULPTURES

The artist Erwin Wurm began his *One Minute Sculptures* in 1988, and has since been continuously contributing to the encyclopaedic series in myriad locations around the world. The artist directs volunteers to interact in paradoxical ways with random everyday objects – a chair, pencils, fresh fruit – for around one minute, standing still as Wurm takes their photo.

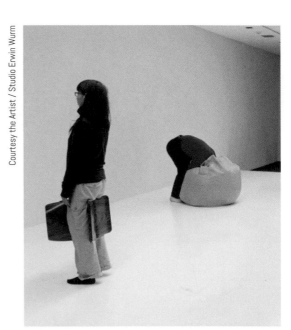

Courtesy the Artist / Studio Erwin Wurm

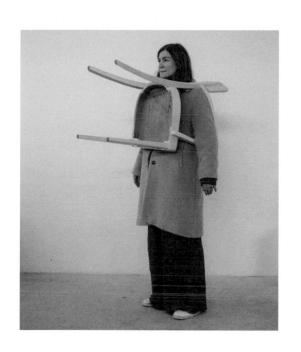
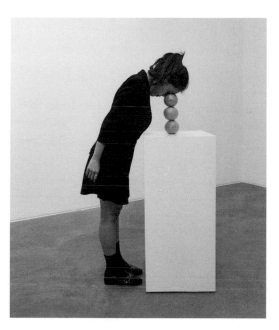

CONSTRAINTS

DRAW WITH A BLINDFOLD

Or draw a subject you can see (flowers, a still life, etc.) on paper hidden from your sight.

DRAW WHILE ARM WRESTLING

Or performing some other physical task, or draw upwards, i.e. while lying underneath a table, or with your left hand.

DRAW TO ORDER

Find someone else to draw what you want.

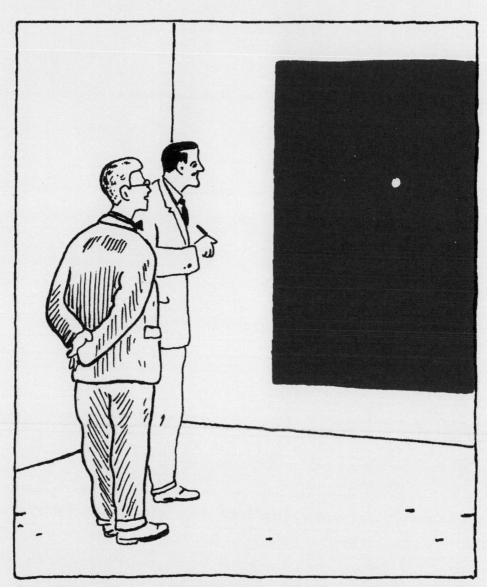

"1 THINK 1 PREFER HIS EARLIER, LESS OVERTLY FIGURATIVE WORK"

Glen Baxter, *Ominous Stains*, 2015

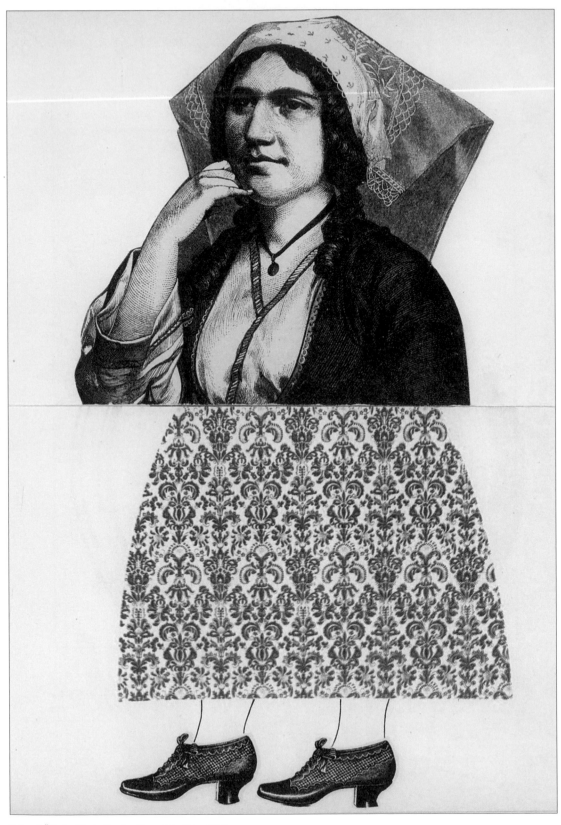

Bohumil Štěpán, illustration for *Crazy Fairy Tales*, 1965

THE EXQUISITE CORPSE

Similar to the game Heads, Bodies and Legs, this is a game in which each participant takes turns drawing on a sheet of paper, folding it to conceal his or her contribution, and then passing it to the next player for a further contribution. The game gained popularity in creative circles during the 1920s when it was adopted as a technique by artists of the Surrealist movement to generate collaborative compositions.

POSTCARD PLAY

Artists are often fascinated by postcards, which are ready-made images; it is very tempting to subvert their predictable repertoire of images and spark new meaning. In many cases this is done simply by adding new elements.

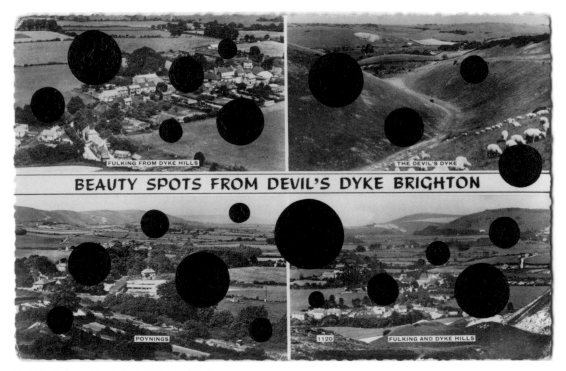

David Bellingham, *(Beauty Spots), Brighton*, 2019

MEMORY MAPS

Drawn or painted, created with printed ephemera to make a collage, or made from some other materials, memory maps are a fascinating creative device. Recall a childhood room, house or garden and compare your map with those who share the memory: differences between one and another may be revelatory.

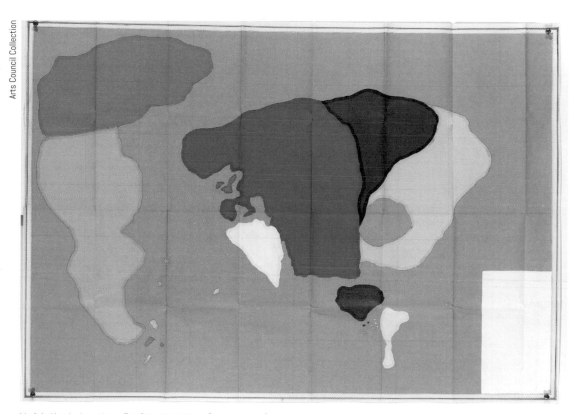

Mariele Neudecker, *Never Eat Shredded Wheat (Memory Maps), Drawn by 32-year-old Italian Female*, 1996

DAILY PLAY

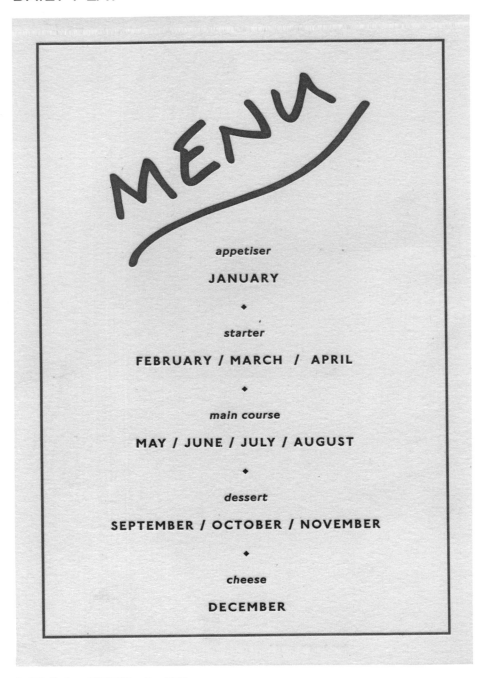

MENU

appetiser

JANUARY

◆

starter

FEBRUARY / MARCH / APRIL

◆

main course

MAY / JUNE / JULY / AUGUST

◆

dessert

SEPTEMBER / OCTOBER / NOVEMBER

◆

cheese

DECEMBER

David Bellingham, *WAX366 New Year*, 2017

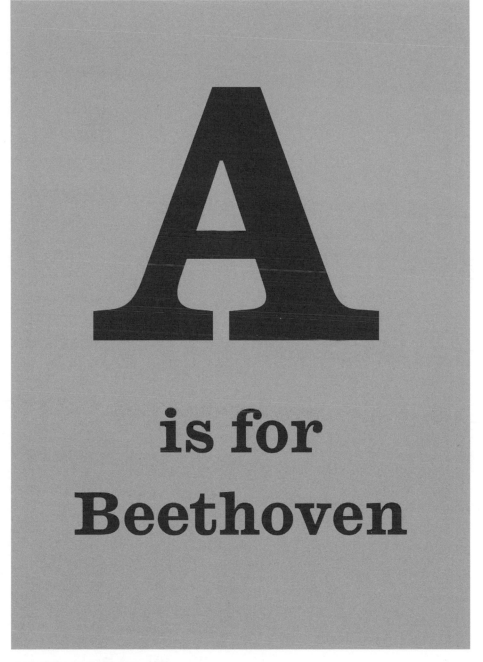

Jeremy Deller, *A is for Beethoven*, 2020

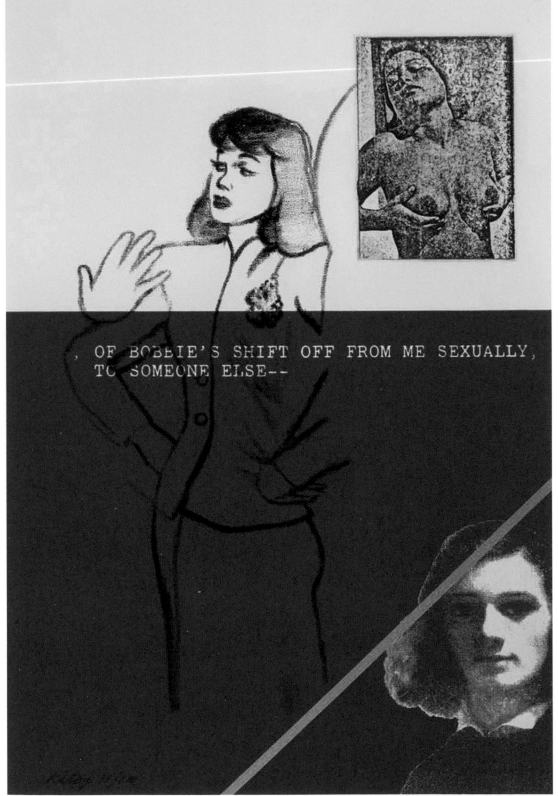

R. B. Kitaj, *A Day Book (Ramkalawon 133–146)*, 1970–72

PICTURE POEMS

The idea here is to use collage to create a poem – with or without words. To do this, you bring together diverse visual materials to make an image in which connections, repetitions or visual rhymes, present a poetic story or record a significant event. The poem might be about a weekend spent in a particular place, a memorable or important journey, a love affair, a person you love or admire, or anything else that interests you.

MODIFYING PHOTOGRAPHS

This Polish artist and photographer manipulates archival photographs to create something new and disconcerting.

Weronika Gęsicka, *Untitled #1*, from the series Traces, 2015–17

TOY-MAKING

A kind of assemblage made by using disparate elements often scavenged by the artist, but sometimes bought specially.

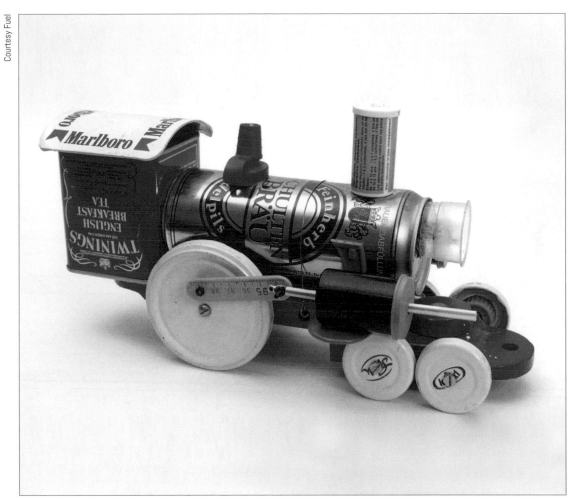

Aleksandr Chebotaryov, a toy train made for the artist's son, 1996, from the book *Home Made* by Vladimir Arkhipov

COLLECTING

Now the problem with a collection is realising that you've started one. Recently I have begun, quite unintentionally, to collect old postcards thematically. It started with finding an attractive postcard of a frozen water fountain. On finding the second frozen water fountain, I had begun a collection …

You've started so you must continue, and with most collections, there is no end. Whether it is postcards of lighthouses or four-leaf clovers, there can never be the definitive collection. For what is more inert than a finished collection?

From Tacita Dean, 'Collections', Museu d'Art Contemporary de Barcelona (MACBA), *Tacita Dean*, 2000

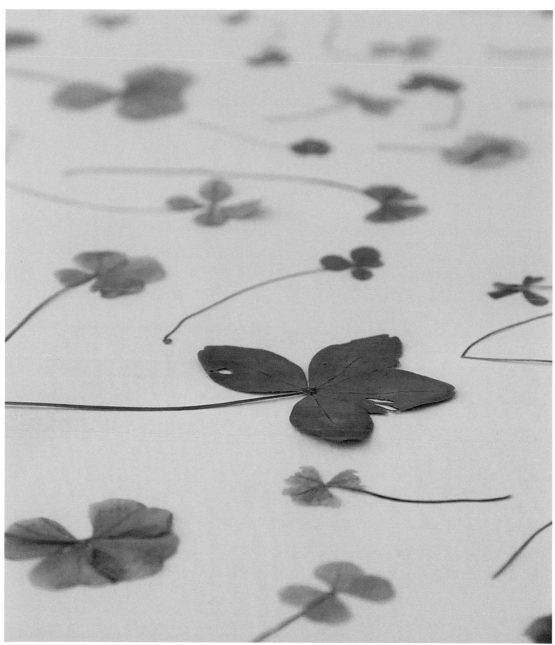

Tacita Dean, *Four, Five, Six, Seven and Nine Leaf Clover Collection* (detail), 1972–present

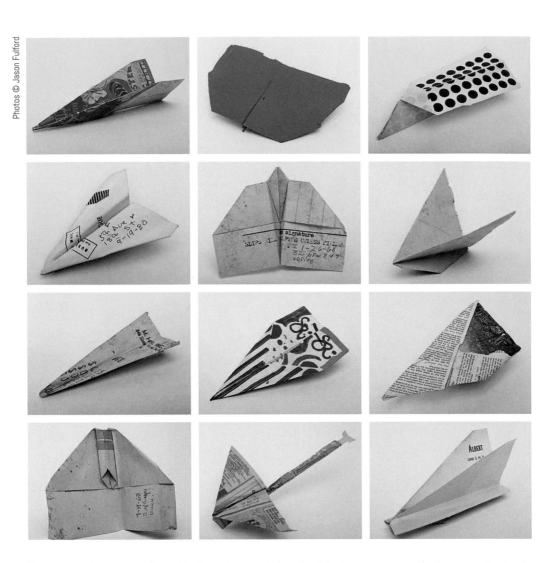

These paper planes were collected by the artist Harry Smith who picked up every paper plane he saw on the streets of Manhattan from 1961 to 1983. These were haphazardly folded from homework, a Betty Crocker cookbook, a Heineken label, an anti-war rally flyer, receipts, and a Max's Kansas City menu.

From John Klacsmann and Andrew Lampert, eds, *Paper Airplanes: The Collections of Harry Smith Catalogue Raisonné, Volume I*, 2015

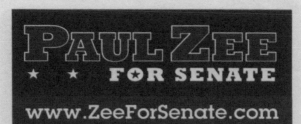

www.ZeeForSenate.com

DRAINO

PLUNGER

RCA CABLES

PEACHES

BATH TUB SCRUB
BRUSH

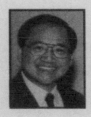

"I want all children who graduate from California schools to know how to read, write and speak English."

Paul Zee
City Councilmember/Businessman
(626) 403-7777

Ephemera found by David Shrigley

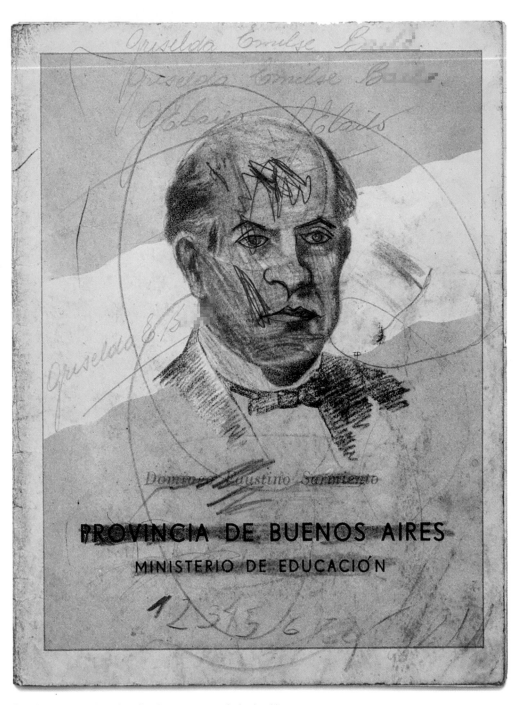

PROVINCIA DE BUENOS AIRES

MINISTERIO DE EDUCACIÓN

Exercise book cover from the collection at www.exercisebookarchive.org

TAUCHNITZ EDITION

COLLECTION OF BRITISH AND AMERICAN AUTHORS

VOL. 5027

THE ENGLISH: ARE THEY HUMAN?

BY

G. J. RENIER

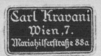

LEIPZIG: BERNHARD TAUCHNITZ

PARIS: LIBRAIRIE GAULON & FILS, 39, RUE MADAME

Not to be introduced into the British Empire and U.S.A.

Book cover, 1932 from the Redstone Press collection

VISUAL POEMS

The Catalan artist, poet, playwright and magician Joan Brossa was a leading proponent of visual poetry.

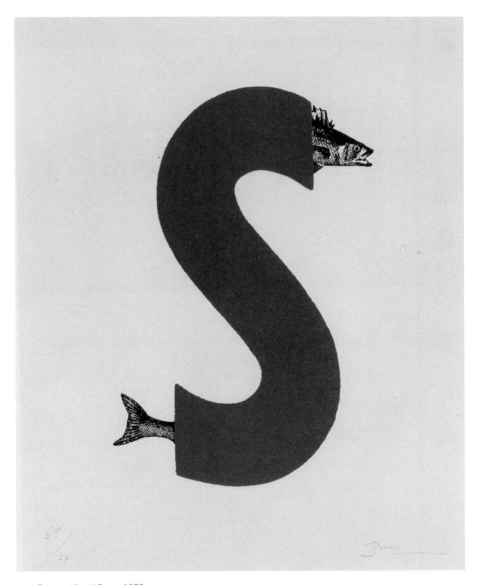

Joan Brossa, *Visual Poem*, 1978

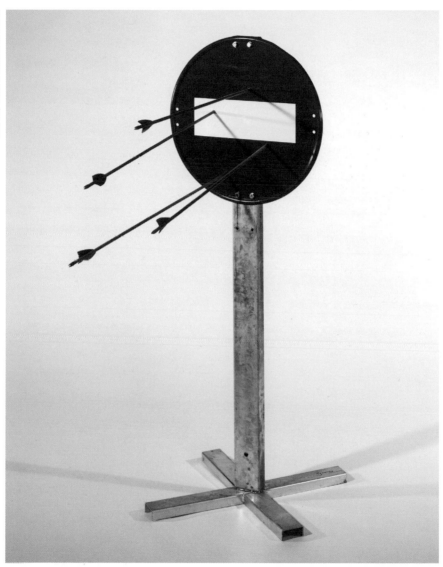

Joan Brossa, *Do Not Pass*, 1988

TRANSFORMED BOOKS

MEL GOODING

From ancient times the book has been regarded as a sacred object. It is the container of Wisdom, the repository of Authority, the preserver of History, the transmitter of Custom and the Law. The book as an object is a potent symbol of all that is of consequence in a literate culture. Books keep the world the right way up. Defacing, deforming, vandalising, destroying, burning, trashing, or otherwise transforming books are shocking Crimes against the Order of Things as They Are and Should Be. They are not merely acts of wilful damage: they are acts of symbolic anarchy. They turn the world upside down. When we encounter such transgressions we laugh nervously.

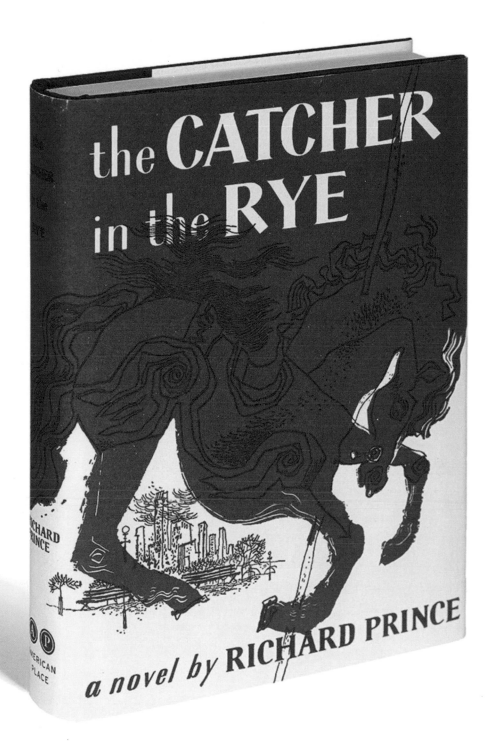

Richard Prince, *The Catcher in the Rye*, 2011
This is an artwork by Richard Prince. Any similarity to a book is coincidental and not intended by the artist.
A facsimile of the first edition of J. D. Salinger's novel in which Prince replaces Salinger's name with his own.

THUS the heavens and the earth were finiſhed, and all the hoſt of them.

2 And on the ſeventh day God ended his work which he had made; and he reſted on the ſeventh day from all his work which he had made.

3 And God bleſſed the ſe-venth day, and ſanctified it: becauſe that in it he had reſted from all his work which God created and made.

Alfred Woods, page from his colour-coded Macklin Bible, 1888–1900

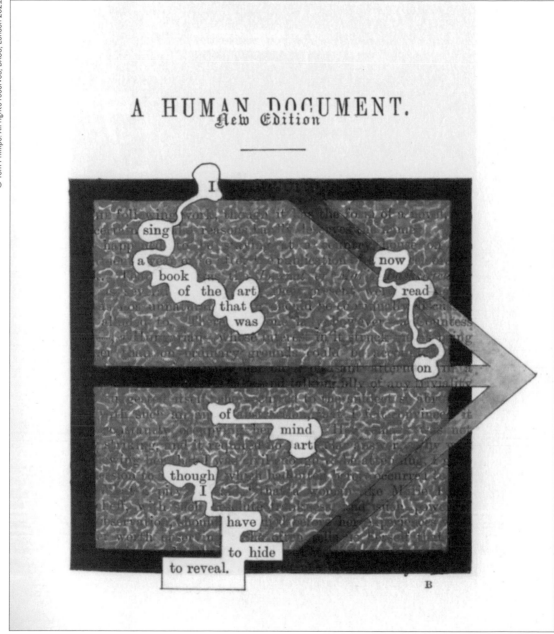

Tom Phillips, title page from *A Humument*, an ongoing project started in 1973

"Can I go to my room?" says John.

"No, I have donated it to all the victims of colonial-imperialism," says Mummy. "They are moving in tomorrow."

new words colonial charity bedroom

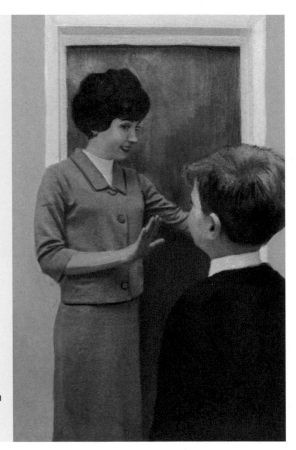

Miriam Elia, from a series of spoof Ladybird books, 2013

John is painting a picture.

"You must paint your inner child," says Mummy.

"But I am a child," says John.

new words repressed inner adult

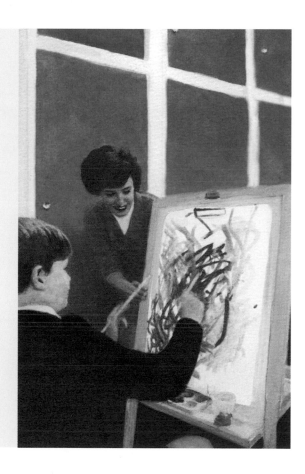

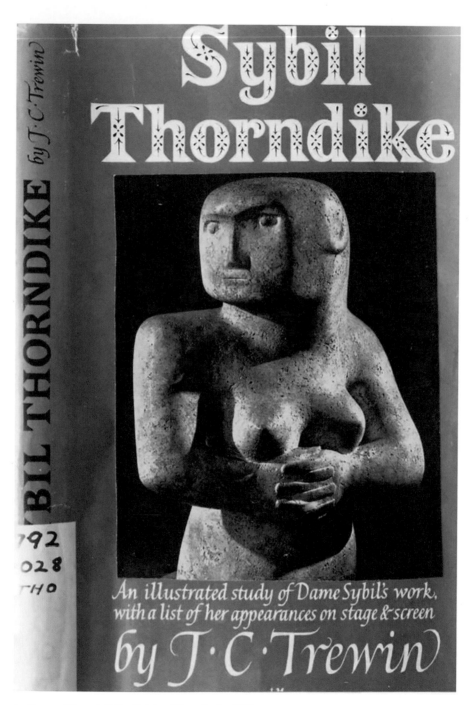

Joe Orton and Kenneth Halliwell, defaced library books, 1960s

The playwright Joe Orton and his boyfriend, later murderer, Kenneth Halliwell were appalled by the selection of books available at their local library and protested by giving the book new cover pictures and blurbs. They were caught by the police who wrote alleging an illegally parked car, provoking an incandescent reply from Halliwell lambasting the petty-mindedness of the council and pointing out that they did not have a car. The police had got what they wanted – a typed letter which matched the typeface of text on the book jackets.

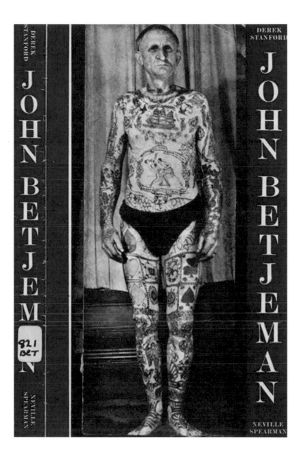

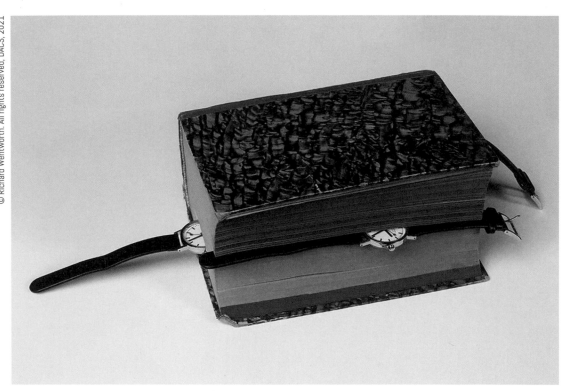

Richard Wentworth, *Time and Place*, 2004

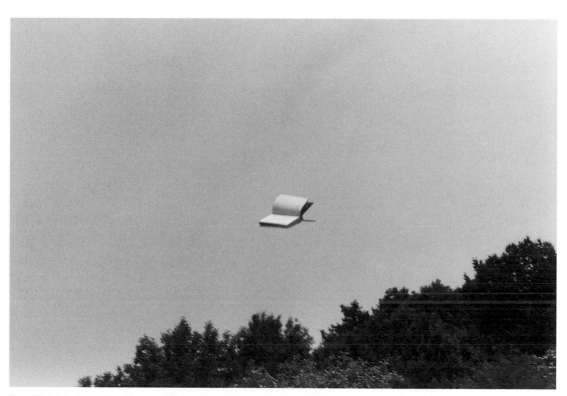

Peter Wüthrich, *Return-Here, There and Everywhere*, 1994. A book thrown into the air becomes a flying book

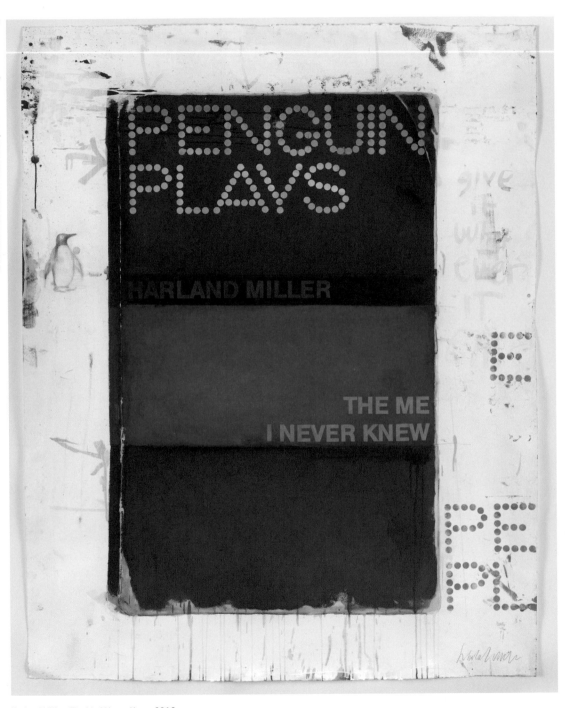

Harland Miller, *The Me I Never Knew*, 2018

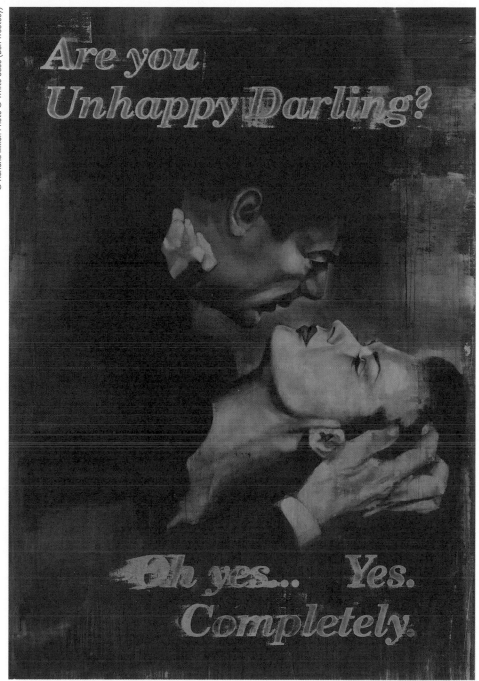

Harland Miller, *Painting for Charles Addams*, 2012

FORGOTTEN BOOKS

Library card catalogues have become obsolete in most institutions. The artist David Bunn rescued two million of these catalogue cards from the Los Angeles Central Library, and uses them to create marvellous poems and other works of art.

The forgotten arts: cooking without fuel.

641.588   Older, Julia, 1941–

641.48   The Forgotten art of making old-fashioned
F721   pickles, relishes, chutneys, sauces and
            catsups, mincemeats, beverages, and
            syrups: one hundred and thirty-six
            treasured family recipes, selected
            from the thousands submitted to the
            Old farmer's almanac and Yankee magazine

            The forgotten art of growing, gardening,
635.7   and cooking with herbs.

            The forgotten art of flower cookery.
641.659   Smith, Leona Woodring.
S654

            The forgotten art of building a
                stone wall.
693.1   Fields, Curtis P
F461   The forgotten art of building a stone
            wall; an illustrated guide to dry wall
            construction. Dublin, N. H., Yankee,
            c1971.

            The forgotten art of building a good fireplace.
697.1   Orton, Vrest, 1897–
O 78a   Observations on the forgotten art of building
            a good fireplace.

            The forgotten art of building a good
697.1   fireplace.
O 78   Orton, Vrest, 1897–
              Observations on the forgotten art of
            building a good fireplace.

David Bunn, *The Forgotten Art*, 2011

SORTED BOOKS

Nina Katchadourian began her project in 1993 and it continues to this day. The process is always the same: the artist goes through a collection of books, chooses particular titles, and eventually groups the books into clusters so that the titles can be read in sequence.

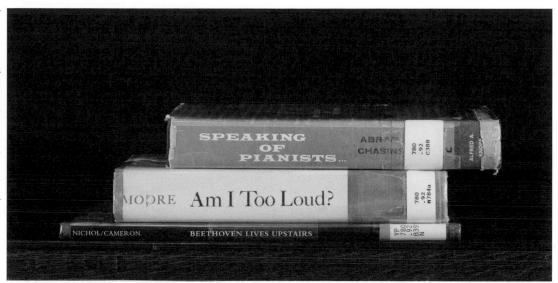

Nina Katchadourian, *Am I Too Loud?*, 1996

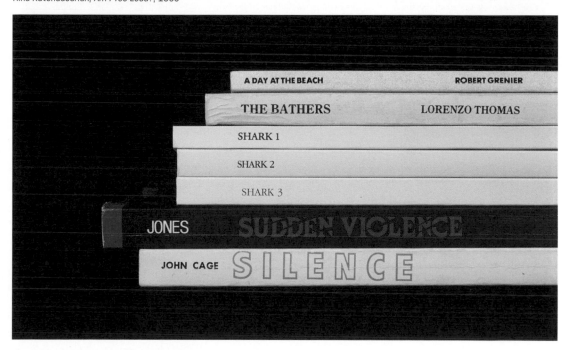

Nina Katchadourian, *A Day at the Beach*, 2001

A BOOK TO BE PLANTED

Please Plant This Book is Richard Brautigan's self-published poetry publication. It consists of a folded and glued folder containing eight seed packets. On the front of each is a poem.

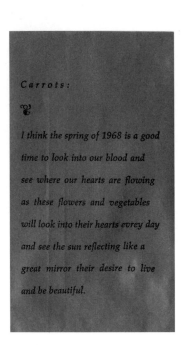

Carrots:

I think the spring of 1968 is a good time to look into our blood and see where our hearts are flowing as these flowers and vegetables will look into their hearts evrey day and see the sun reflecting like a great mirror their desire to live and be beautiful.

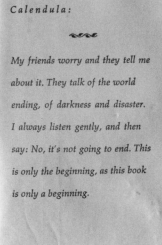

Calendula:

My friends worry and they tell me about it. They talk of the world ending, of darkness and disaster. I always listen gently, and then say: No, it's not going to end. This is only the beginning, as this book is only a beginning.

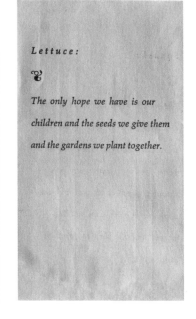

Lettuce:

The only hope we have is our children and the seeds we give them and the gardens we plant together.

Richard Brautigan, *Please Plant This Book*, 1970

*California Native
Flowers:*

೪

*In this spring of 1968 with the last
third of the Twentieth Century
travelling like a dream toward its
end, it is the time to plant books,
to pass them into the ground, so that
flowers and vegetables may grow
from these pages.*

Shasta Daisy:

೪

*I pray that in thirty-two years
passing that flowers and vegetables
will water the Twenty-First Century with their voices telling that
they were once a book turned by
loving hands into life.*

Squash:

೪

*The time is right to mix sentences
sentences with dirt and the sun
with punctuation and the rain with
verbs, and for worms to pass
through question marks, and the
stars to shine down on budding
nouns, and the dew to form on
paragraphs.*

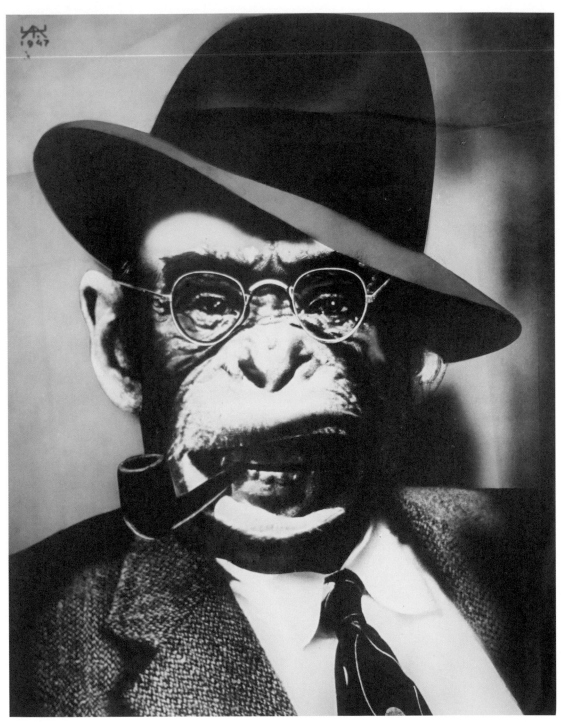

A. Zhitomirsky, *Untitled*, 1947

PROPOSALS

VELIMIR KHLEBNIKOV

Grow edible microscopic organisms in lakes. Every lake will become a kettle of readymade soup that only needs to be heated. Contented people will lie about on the shores, swimming and having dinner. The food of the future.

Effect the exchange of labour and services by means of an exchange of heartbeats. Estimate every task in terms of heartbeats – the monetary unit of the future, in which all individuals are equally wealthy. Take 365 x 317 as the median number of heartbeats in any twenty-four hour period.

Devise the art of waking easily from dreams.

Adopt apes into the family of man and grant them selected rights of citizenship.

Set aside a special uninhabited island, such as Iceland, for a never-ending war between anybody from any country who wants to fight now (for people who want to die like heroes).

Redesign chemical and biological warfare so that it merely puts people to sleep. Then governments will earn our admiration and deserve our praise.

Let factory chimneys awake and sing morning hymns to the rising sun, above the Seine as well as over Tokyo, over the Nile, and over Delhi.

Create a new occupation – penmen – recognizing that the graphic quiver of handwriting itself has a powerful effect on the reader. The unheard voice of handwriting. Also create a recognised class of artists who work with numbers.

Utilise the boring eyes of trains as projectors for flashing out schedules of what's happening tomorrow in the arts, like an arrow in swift pursuit.

From Charlotte Douglas, ed, *The Collected Works of Velimir Khlebnikov, Vol. 1: Letters and Theoretical Writings*, 1987. Translated by Paul Schmidt, 1987

MLADEN STILINOVIĆ

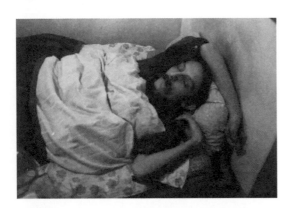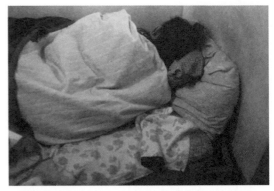

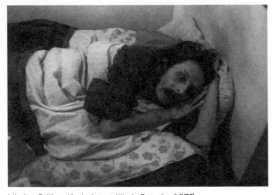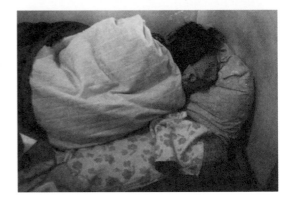

Mladen Stilinović, *Artist at Work*, Croatia, 1977

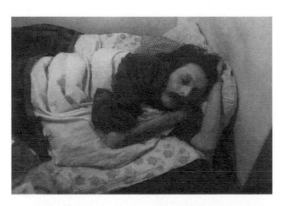
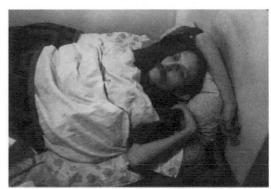
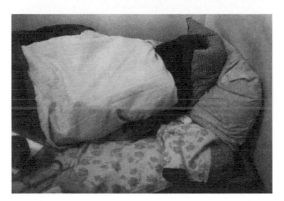
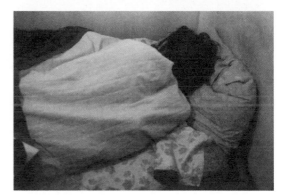

ANDREI MONASTYRSKI

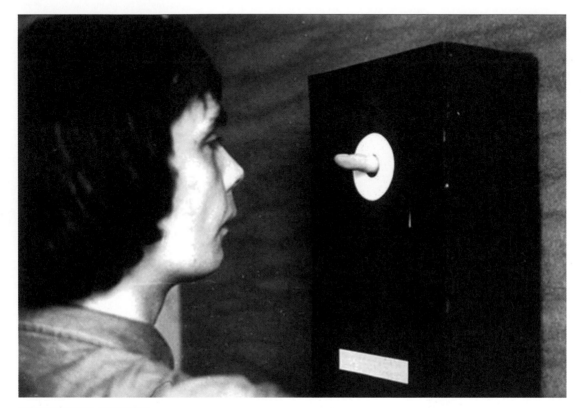

Andrei Monastyrski, *Finger*, 1977

A black, elongated vertical box without a bottom is fixed to the wall. A round hole has been made in the upper half of the box's facing side. The lower half of the facing side contains a label with the following text:

A finger, or an indication of oneself as an object external to oneself

Anyone who wishes to participate in the action puts their hand into the box from below, and through the round hole in the upper half of the front wall points his index finger towards himself.

JOHN GIORNO

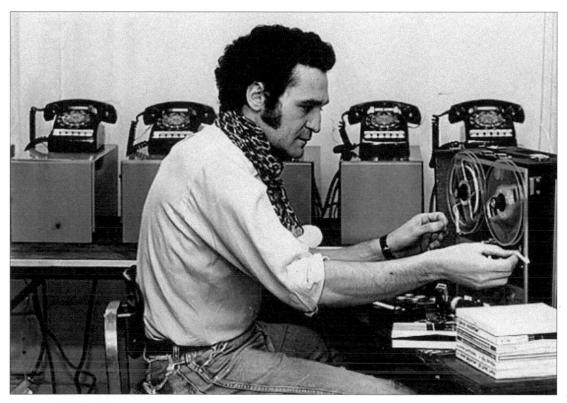

John Giorno at *Dial-a-Poem*, 1969

The artist and activist John Giorno set up *Dial-a-Poem* with fifteen rotary telephones in a room at the Architectural League rigged up to a bank of bulky recording devices. There were fifteen answering machines for each of the phones, which you could call from anywhere and listen to a poem, speech, comedy or sound art, at random. Stickers advertising the phone number were placed in public phone booths, in cafés, on bulletin boards and on the subways so the listener could hear Patti Smith, William Burroughs and other great countercultural figures of the time.

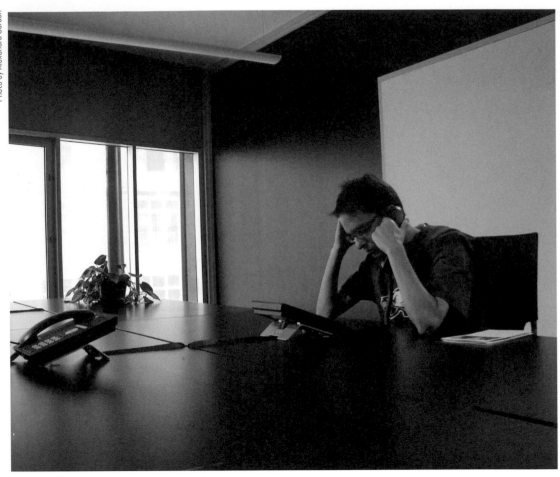

Installation view at the Contemporary Art Museum St Louis, 2009

CAREY YOUNG

This artist mimics the typical call centre experience, through which she offers access to a bizarre imaginary museum. Callers must negotiate a labyrinthine sonic hypertext that includes menus and submenus, with options for various departments, recorded information and even the chance to speak with a live staff member.

Some of the departments include:

Death of Painting Revival Team
Office of Pardons
Corporate Laundry
Manifesto Department
Mythic Repository of Spare Ideas
Chair of Disappointing Home Truths
Agency for Repetitive Thinking
Urban Regeneration and Soul Selling team
Trauma Department
Creative Undertaker

Specific activities that can be undertaken by the caller include:
Applying for an internship at the Museum
Leaving a voicemail for the Artist in Residence
Pledging a gift
Speaking with the Operator (a real person)

Also, the Operator is trained to be able to direct the caller to real locations or elements within the exhibition venue, such as the exit, bathrooms or visitors' book.

Carey Young, *Welcome to the Museum*, 2009. Professional call centre agent, script written by the artist, call centre software, direct dial telephone connection, telephone, chair, table, houseplant.

WORKS OF ART TRANSFORMED

SALLY O'REILLY

SIR ROBERT SHIRLEY AND THE FIRE-BACKED PHEASANT

As you can tell from the glint in the pheasant's eye, this is no bird but a man in a costume. These are the commemorative prints of the winner and the runner-up of the fancy dress prize at Werner Heisenberg's twenty-fifth birthday party. A scandal broke when the runner-up, Albert Einstein, was later disqualified after judges were 'informed' by an undisclosed petitioner that this had been a real bird trained to masquerade as a man in costume.

The incident precipitated a spate of copycat crimes. Contestants, instead of dressing up as a public figure, would stay at home and send the actual public figure to the party in their name. There are historical records of one soirée, in February 1927, where a young Greta Garbo claimed to be Prime Minister Stanley Baldwin in drag, and Sylvia and Christabel Pankhurst sent a horse in their stead, scooping the first prize of ten bob, which they never did retrieve from their double-crossing accomplice.

This fad for cheating was short-lived, thanks to the influence of Hollywood's sleazy tabloids. One could never be sure if the celebrity one sent wouldn't behave appallingly and drag one's own name through very public mud. An unexpected consequence of note from this period, however, was the profound uncertainty that Heisenberg would continue to feel.

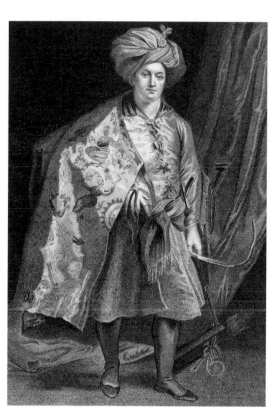

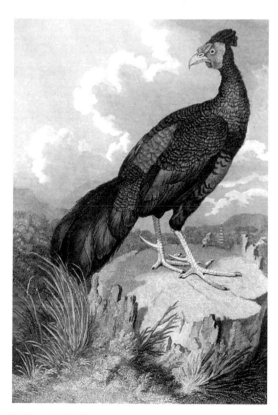

William Nelson Gardiner, *Sir Robert Shirley*, 19th century   S. Edwards, *The Fire-Backed Pheasant of Java*, 1796

ART CLASS ASSIGNMENTS

JOHN BALDESSARI

Make up an art game. Structure a set of rules with which to play. A physical game is not necessary; more important are the rules and their structure. Do we in life operate by rules? Does all art? Or art rules, like tenant rules or art violations.

How can plants be used in art. Problem becomes how can we really get people to look freshly at plants as if they've never noticed them before. A few possibilities: 1. Arrange them alphabetically like books on a shelf; 2. Plant them like popsicle trees (as in child art) perpendicular to line of hill; 3. Include object among plants that is camouflaged; 4. Colour palm tree pink; 5. Photo found growing arrangements; 6. Or a movie on How to Plant a Plant.

One person copies or makes-up random captions. Another person takes photos. Match photos to captions.

Disguise an object to look like another object.

Document change, decay, metamorphosis, changes occurring in time. Photograph same thing at various times during the day.

Photograph backs of things, underneaths of things, extreme foreshortenings, uncharacteristic views. Or trace them.

Describe the visual verbally and the verbal visually.

Repaired or patched art. Recycled. Find something broken and discarded. Perhaps in a thrift store. Mend it.

These ideas come from the preparatory materials for Baldessari's *Cal Arts Post Studio Art: Class Assignments*, 1970

TIPS FOR ARTISTS WHO WANT TO SELL

- GENERALLY SPEAKING, PAINT-INGS WITH LIGHT COLORS SELL MORE QUICKLY THAN PAINTINGS WITH DARK COLORS.

- SUBJECTS THAT SELL WELL : MADONNA AND CHILD, LANDSCAPES, FLOWER PAINTINGS, STILL LIFES (FREE OF MORBID PROPS ___ DEAD BIRDS, ETC.), NUDES, MARINE PICTURES, ABSTRACTS AND SUR-REALISM.

- SUBJECT MATTER IS IMPOR - TANT: IT HAS BEEN SAID THAT PA-INTINGS WITH COWS AND HENS IN THEM COLLECT DUST ___ WHILE THE SAME PAINTINGS WITH BULLS AND ROOSTERS SELL.

John Baldessari, *Tips for Artists Who Want to Sell*, 1966–68. The painting is realised by sign painters with text taken from an art manual offering advice on subject matter.

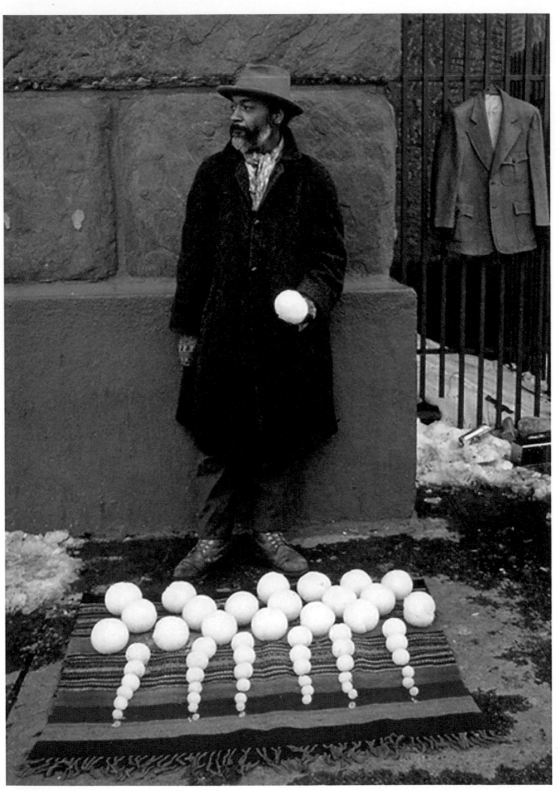

David Hammons, *Bliz-aard Ball Sale, Cooper Square, New York,* 1983

ACTIVITIES

ELIZABETH DEMARAY

This American artist developed the *Lichen for Skyscrapers* project and writes: 'One of the ways to reduce heat in these cities is to cultivate lichen, which forms a protective barrier, insulating its supporting building from harmful elements. It can lower cumulative temperatures by absorbing sunlight and reflecting heat due to its light colour palate while making oxygen and creating green space on the sides of buildings.'

Other projects include *Alternative Housing for Hermit Crabs* (2000) and *The Endangered Species Recipe Book: Animals that Have Gone Extinct or Are Going Extinct and The Recipes that We Have Used to Eat Them* (2014).

NINA KATCHADOURIAN

This American artist suggested parking cars in different car parks only according to their colour. To generate awareness and enthusiasm for the event, the artist mounted a huge informational campaign with video, posters and announcements read in schools. Thousands of cars were flyered in the days previous to the event so that drivers would know the easiest place to park based on their car colour. The white lot was the largest (17% of cars in San Diego were white), with red as the runner-up (13%). This became the project called *Carpark* (1994). No one could find their car at the end of the day.

EMMA KAY

This British artist is interested in individual memory and how it processes maps, literature, religion and the past: the stuff of shared understanding. Her book *Worldview* (2000) is precisely that, an idiosyncratic global history drawn exclusively from half-remembered exams, costume dramas and articles from colour supplements. *The Bible from Memory* (1997) was her first text using only her own recall, and was followed by *Shakespeare from Memory* (1999).

ADAM DANT'S URBAN ACTIVITIES

1. Start an argument with a friend on a busy bus about the places you anticipate passing en route, adding all manner of fictitious landmarks; the Albert Aqueduct; the Children's Prison, etc. The winner is decided by the number of other passengers who pretend to recognise any of these made-up places as real.

2. Superimpose a map from one city to another, and use it to navigate the streets. This can be repeated with kitchen plans, wiring diagrams and pictures of the moon or night sky.

3. Stick a pin through a point in the A to Z guide where you are standing, then make the journey from there to the place where the pin comes through on the other side of the page.

4. Pay a violin player or other busker to follow you around the city. Walk in time with music.

5. Create a big opaque ink stain on, or a tear a hole in, your map of the city. Ask strangers to fill in the obscured bit by drawing the missing streets on a piece of paper. Perform this exercise until the whole map has been reimagined by the city's inhabitants.

6. Planning consultation: write the words 'MONUMENT REMOVAL COMMITTEE' onto a binder file and, wearing a high-viz vest bearing the same words, start recording the dimensions of the plinths of various statues with a tape measure.

7. Visit a museum and view it as a shop, the shop as a museum, guards as guides, curators as caretakers, visitors as the exhibits, etc.

8. In the early morning, arrange the remnants of a bonfire (burnt twigs etc.) in the middle of the town square with various chewed animal bones strewn around. Put it about via posters and gossip that a tribe of mysterious savage cavepeople have arrived in town.

MAP PIECE

Draw a map to get lost.

1964 spring

Yoko Ono, *Map Piece*, 1964

SELMA SELMAN

This artist and activist is from Bosnia-Herzegovina. As part of her practice she dismantles whole cars and smashes washing machines and vacuum cleaners in public performances.

(video length: 13 minutes). Photo documentation: Tibor Varga Somogyi

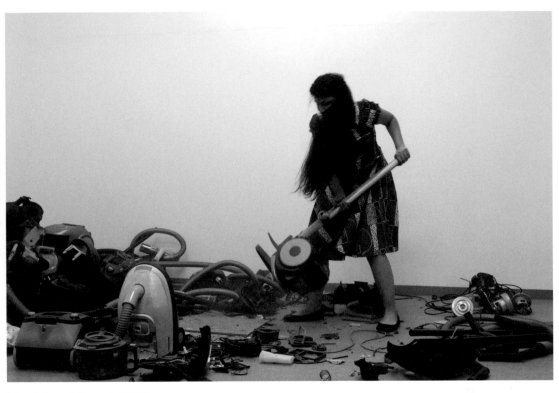

Selma Selman, *Self portrait II*, 2017

ANNA AND BERNHARD BLUME

These two German artists were pioneers of staged photography and often used their work to subvert the idea of Home Sweet Home.

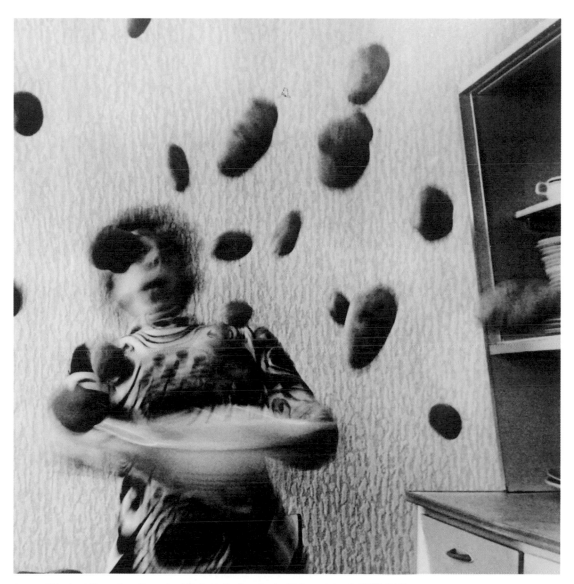

Anna and Bernhard Blume, from the series *Kürchenkoller* (an attack of flying potatoes), 1985–2016

KIRSTEN PIEROTH

German artist Kirsten Pieroth pumped a Berlin street puddle into water canisters and relocated the puddle in Albania by pouring the water out in an exhibition space of the First Tirana Bienniale.

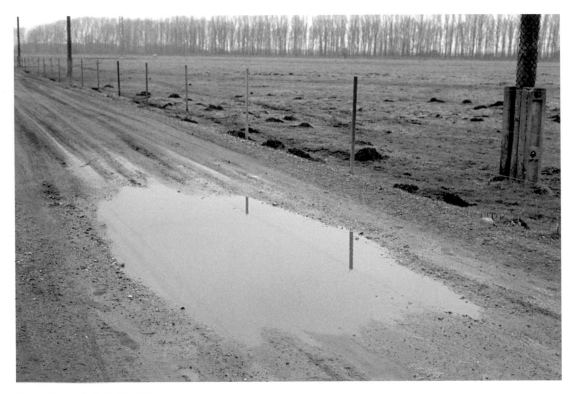

Kirsten Pieroth, *Berlin Puddle*, 2001

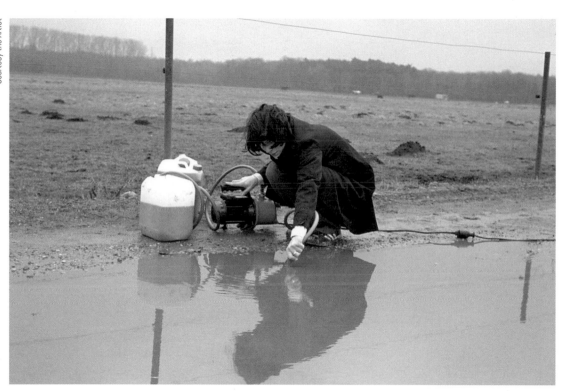

For *Memoirs of a Puddle* turn to page 163

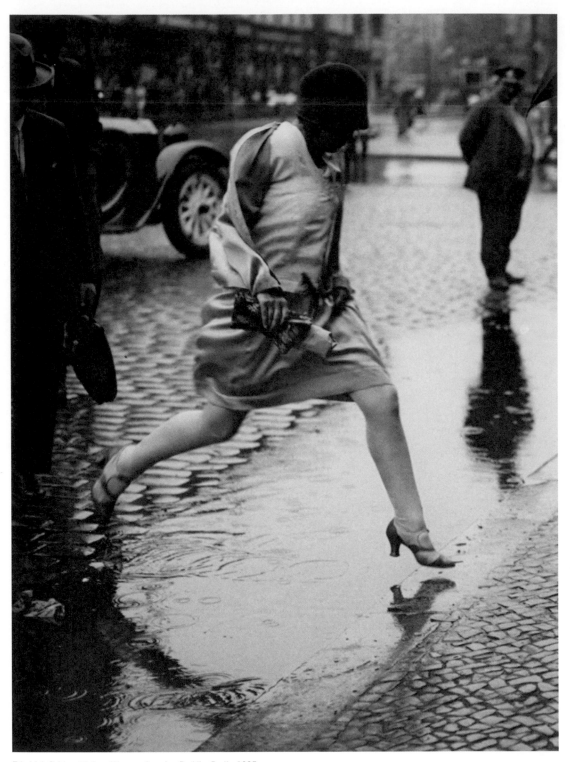

Friedrich Seidenstücker, *Woman Jumping Puddle, Berlin*, 1925

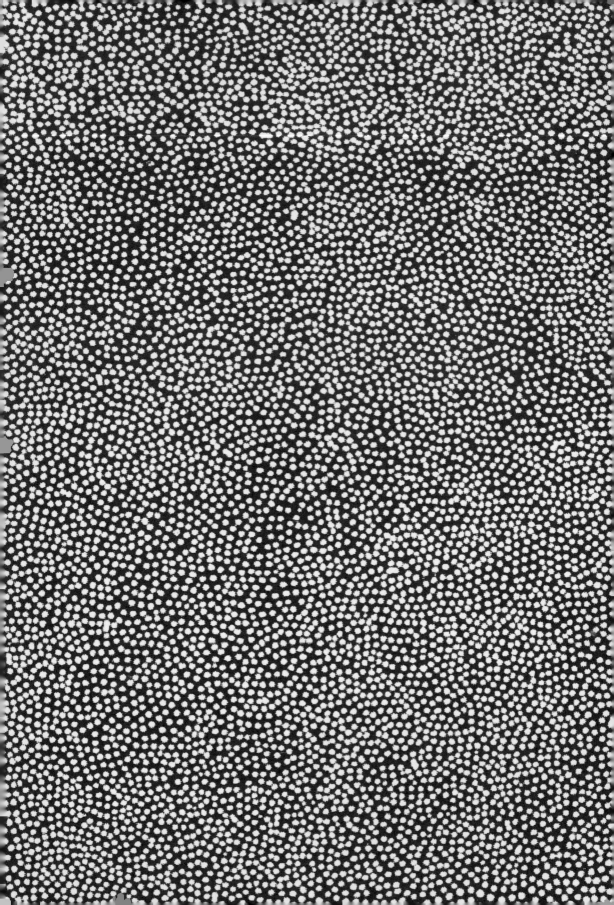

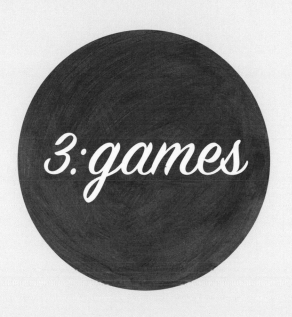

3:games

Games, so strictly governed by rules, yet essentially unproductive and frivolous, should be taken seriously. Not like Ann Margret in *The Cincinatti Kid* who alters a jigsaw piece with a nail file. Asked why, she says, 'So it'll fit, Stupid.'

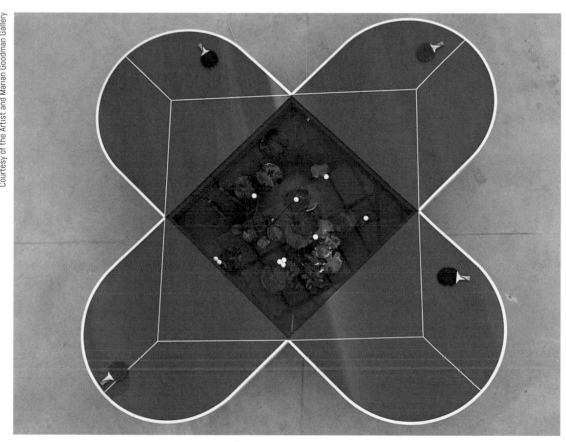

Gabriel Orozco, *Ping Pond Table* (modified ping pong tables, water lilies, water, mixed media), 1998

DANGEROUS GAMES

'Let's play wake the dead!'

'Wake the Dead! Can I play?'

'What do I need?'

'Did you bring a shovel?'

The Addams Family, 1991

'Mary,' she screamed, 'come on up here.'

When Mary arrived in the tower, Christina asked her

if she would not like to play a very special game with her.

'It's called "I forgive you for all your sins."'

Jane Bowles, *Two Serious Ladies*, 1943

CRICKET

You have two sides, one out in the field and one in. Each man that's in the side that's in goes out, and when he's out he comes in and the next man goes in until he's out.

When they are all out, the side that's out comes in and the side thats been in goes out and tries to get those coming in, out. Sometimes you got men still in and not out.

When a man goes out to go in, the men who are out try to get him out, and when he is out he goes in and the next man in goes out and goes in. There are two men called umpires who stay all out all the time and they decide when the men who are in are out.

When both sides have been in and all the men have been out, and both sides have been out twice after all the men have been in, including those who are not out, that is the end of the game!

The rules of cricket explained, sometimes attributed to the Marylebone Cricket Club

DOZENS: A GAME OF INSULTS

A game of put-downs: the rapid, ritualistic exchange of insults, often targeting family members. The rhetorical contest of playing or shooting the dozens (also known as capping, ranking, and sounding) is most commonly practised by young, urban African American males. A good dozens player not only coolly withstands merciless insults to his family; he also twists memorised insults quickly to suit the opponent at hand.

Your mama's so FAT, after she got off the carousel, the horse limped for a week.

Your mama's so skinny, she can hula-hoop through a Froot Loop.

Your mama's so FAT, her blood type is Ragu.

Your mama's so skinny, she looks like a mic stand.

Your mama's so FAT, instead of 501 jeans she wears 1002s.

Your mama's so skinny, she turned sideways and disappeared.

Your mama's so FAT she's not on a diet she's on a triet. *What y'all eating? I'll try it.*

Your mama's so skinny, I gave her a piece of popcorn and she went into a coma.

Your mama's so FAT, when she jumped in the air she got stuck.

Your mama's so skinny, you could blindfold her with dental floss.

Mo'nique Imes and Sherry A. McGee, *Skinny Women Are Evil: Notes of a Big Girl in a Small-Minded World*, 2004

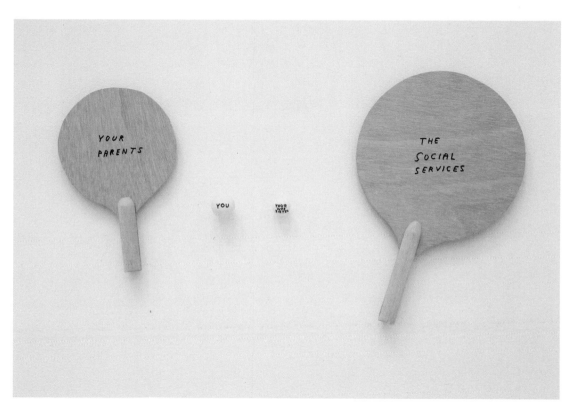

David Shrigley, *You, Your Wee Sister, Your Parents and Social Services*, 2001

THE COMIC GAME

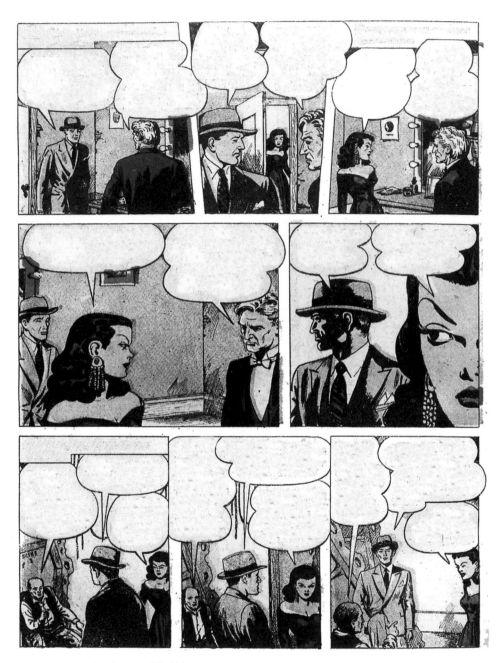

Invent new text for the speech bubbles.

THE BOOK GAME

Choose a book from the shelf. Read the title and the description on the back cover to the players, who then have to guess what the first line of the book might be. Each player writes down their guess on a separate piece of paper; as well as the correct first line.

All the texts are gathered and read aloud by the person who has chosen the book. Points are then given for the best first line and to anyone who chooses the correct entry.

THE EDIBLE BOOK GAME

Players must create an edible dish which references a piece of literature either explicitly or using a play on words. Play this game at home with family, or hold a small gathering for foodies and bibliophiles. Choose your winner by popular vote and participants should then enjoy eating the submissions.

Examples include: 'Scone with the wind', 'Why I'm no longer talking to white people about rice', 'Chow mein kampf', 'Cream and punishment'.

Conceived by Judith A. Hoffberg and Béatrice Coron in 2000

THE DICTIONARY GAME

Take it in turns to pick a word from the dictionary, write out its definition, and then invent two more definitions of your own. Then read the three possible definitions out to the group — or get your neighbour to do so if you have a bad poker face. The others must each guess which is the true definition. One point for anyone who spots the real one, and two points for you if one of your fake ones is voted the winner.

THE PORTRAIT GAME

This game was invented by Ivan Turgenev. He would sketch portraits of imaginary people, whose characters he and his friends would then describe. The Portrait Game was first played in 1856 at the Château de Courtavenel, the country house of Louis and Pauline Viardot (an internationally celebrated mezzo-soprano with whom Turgenev was in love).

Young seminary student who has for all the aptitude for the clerical estate a certain amount of cunning. Rather observant, clever, thirsty to learn – he adores women but in an offensive way. It's an unattractive nature, morose, disbelieving in the good – he does not detest the bad. No staunchness – no perseverence – he'll never be a priest. He will end up as a little tutor of youths whom he will turn into perverted creatures like himself. He is without a conscience.

PAULINE VIARDOT

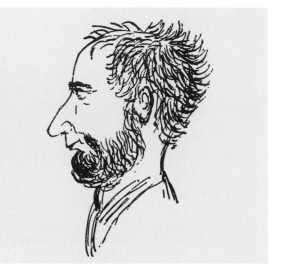

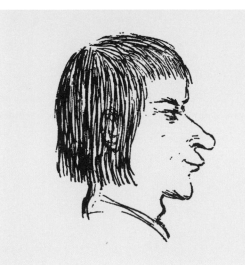

Former bailiff who has lost his best client's fortune at roulette – is meditating suicide or murder, giving the preference to the latter expedient

DR FRISSON

Scion of a family from the Faubourg Saint-Germain who has sunk into sottishness; poor, scrophulous, pious, foolishly gallant, lisping, half dead – has hands cold as icicles, and sweaty – will end a madman. His relatives never mention him save with a compassion that is mingled with disgust.

IVAN TURGENEV

Great Russian landowner, of a noble family; sad-natured, phlegmatic with outbursts of impatience, very honourable, fairly intelligent, cultivated. Likes the theatre, paintings, society, where he says little and listens with a stolid attentiveness. Very conservative.

IVAN TURGENEV

Police inspector, ghastly man – corrupt to the marrow of his bones – all faults – all vices meet in him – If he were not so corpulent, he'd rather like to take up the trade of public executioner ...

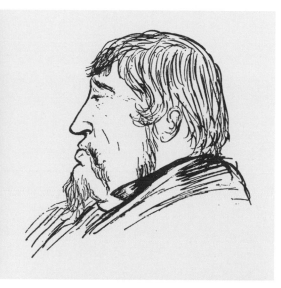

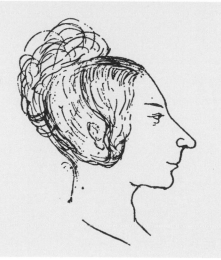

Modest governess in a large family, has charge of several children to whom she isn't managing to teach a thing – weak and timid character. She speaks too low – never looks you in the face – never loses patience. Luke-warm water, slightly sweetened. She's very boring – very honourable, very useless – silent. She hums little sentimental songs like a gnat, accompanying herself – all off – fingers atremble with fear, and never removing her foot from the pedal. She embroiders very nicely – and makes tea exactly according to ritual – is good at sums, but slow. A worthy girl whom people feel sorry for, she's such a bore.

THE BAD ENGLISH GAME

Compete to see who can write a monologue with the most rudimentary grammatical errors and other mistakes. Think about the characteristics of bad English: mistakes of form, spelling, repetition and length; and mistakes of content (nonsensical, unsophisticated, clichéd or stupid). The monologues should be read aloud.

Shoppers are challenged to try and include as many grammatical errors as possible into their interactions with various shop staff with the intention of having these called out and corrected (to win points).

CHINESE WHISPERS

Called Telephone in the United States, this is a game played around the world. One person whispers a message to another, which is passed through a line of people until the last player announces the message to the entire group. Errors typically accumulate in the retellings, so the statement announced by the last player differs significantly, often hilariously, from the one uttered by the first.

THE TRANSLATION GAME

An update of Chinese Whispers, the first player writes two lines of text and translates them into a foreign language using a machine translation site such as Babelfish. The second player then translates them back into English and then into another language by the same means. The game continues until the text reaches the last player, who has to guess the original.

The artist Adam Dant suggests this variation: 1) Buy a random book from an airport bookshop. 2) Translate the title into Spanish and find a passenger to Spain, asking them to find a translation into Arabic at the Madrid–Cairo check-in desk. 3) Make certain someone in Cairo asks for a Russian translation at the Cairo–Moscow desk. 4) Wait at the Arrivals gate for the Chinese–English translation. (This process can be applied to entire novels.)

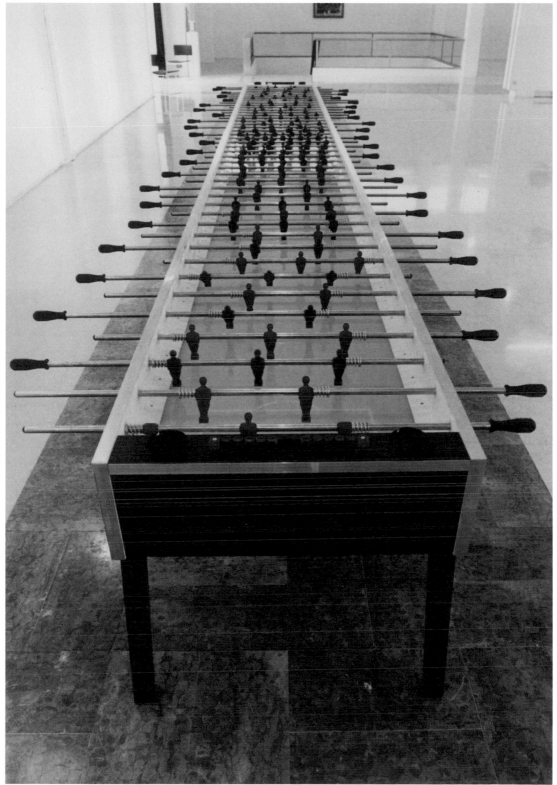

Maurizio Cattelan, *Stadium*, 1991

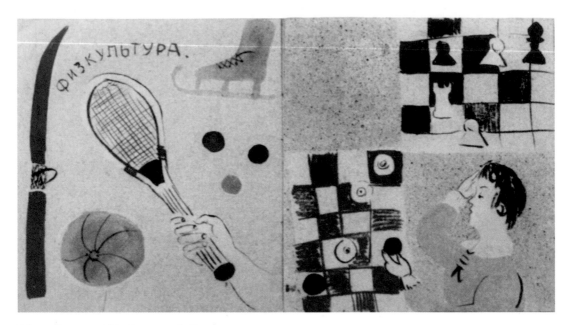

Unknown illustrator, children's games, c.1930

SEKRETIKI

In the late Soviet period, urban children played a game called Sekretiki – little secret treasures. Children – mostly little girls – would gather little objects: flowers, leaves, pretty candy wrappers, ribbons and the like. Then they would search for a nice piece of glass – part of a broken bottle, green, pale blue or transparent. They would dig a little hole in a corner of the courtyard or street where no one could see them, arrange the found objects to make a nice tableau, and then cover it carefully with the glass. They would then pack dirt around this buried picture to hold it in place and sprinkle a fine dusting of sand and dirt over the glass so that no one would notice it. After it was done, they'd invite one or two close friends to come see their Sekretiki. This was something of an honour; you'd only let a close friend see your treasure.

Little boys sometimes made Sekretiki, too, but – according to women who played Sekretiki in their childhoods – the boys usually tried to find their friends' Sekretiki and destroy them.

Michele A. Berdy, *Moscow Times*, 2020

CONSEQUENCES

Players choose a line from a novel that marks the beginning of a dramatic scene. They write the next sentence and pass it on. And so on. When creative depths have been plumbed and no more tales can be spun, read them out.

FAIT DIVERS

Players write a story about a brief news item. Often it will be a tale of the marvellous or the uncanny that would have been reported at length if the participants were better known – best friends turning out to be half-sisters; stick-up men spending their gains on drinks for strangers in a bar; the final thread in a hopelessly tangled web of jealousy and revenge – but it could be anything; it just has to appear in the news media.

As conceived by the playwright Luigi Pirandello.

FORTIFIED CHESS

Identical to conventional chess except for the fact that shot glasses are used as pieces. When a player loses a piece, he or she has to drink the contents. Also known as Occasional Drinker after the line in Raymond Chandler's story, 'The King in Yellow'. *I'm an occasional drinker, the kind of guy who goes out for a beer and wakes up in Singapore with a full beard.*

THE ASSASSIN'S GAME

Players nominate one person to be the detective; he or she in turn chooses an assistant. The detective leaves the room. The remaining players choose an assassin and victim, and hide the hypothetical murder weapon somewhere in the room. The detective comes back in and is blindfolded. Taking the assistant's hand, the detective then walks round the room, trying to identify the criminal, victim and hiding place, with only the pressure of the assistant's hand as guide. A variant has the players choosing a special object – a piece of furniture, a painting, ornament or book – and touching it. The detective then has to come in and guess who has chosen what.

As played by Luis Buñuel.

NAME GAMES

Make sentences or phrases out of people's names – celebrity names or perhaps the names of people you know. Try putting names next to each other and, if possible, have no words in between. You can, however, have a sentence to set you up. For example:

The house is on fire: Googie Withers, George Burns.

The sentences don't have to be spelt correctly, they should just sound funny:

John Hurt Reese Witherspoon
Sebastian Faulks Keira, Knightley
Sid Vicious, Gene Wilder

You might want to include one of these: Glenn Close, Alan Cumming, Diana Quick, Tom Waits, Jimmy Choo, Bono

The writer and performer Sally O'Reilly once belonged to a Punning Club: they would set themselves two themes to play with, such as Food and Authors, generating such gems as:

Edgar Allan Potato, Charles Spotted Dickens, Dan Brown Sauce, Roald Dhal, etc.

THE SECRETS GAME

This game is best played in a large group. Players write down something nobody knows about them on a piece of paper. It doesn't have to be compromising or deeply personal – just an anecdote or piece of trivia that your companions are unfamiliar with. Mix the secrets up in a bag and then read them out one at a time, then vote on whose secret is whose.

THE CONVERSATION GAME

Imagine you're eavesdropping on someone's phone call. Write down one side of a conversation and then read it aloud. Players must write down the other side. These are read aloud and people vote for the best dialogue.

A DINNER PARTY GAME

Before the event, each person is allocated an unusual word or phrase. These words can be assigned by the host or in a circular fashion. Over the course of the gathering, each player's task is to sneak their word or phrase into a conversation without being called out. If you suspect someone of having used the secret word then shout out 'I call ***'. Players get a point for every time they have successfully used their word and a point for every time they have caught someone else in the act.

THE SENTENCE GAME

This is a group game for two or more people. Each player writes ten random words (some of them being commonly used and some unusual) on ten pieces of paper. Each word is allocated a number of points between 1 and 5, depending on the estimated ease of use for the word (e.g. 1 pt for 'and'; 4 pts for 'semiotics'). All words are put in a bag and each player draws eight words.

Within a set time (one minute), every player tries to come up with a sentence consisting of the words drawn. All players read their sentences in turn, and those deemed to make sense by the majority of the players gains points calculated by the sum of the words in their sentence.

QUESTIONS AND ANSWERS

A group game for five or more players. What you need for each player are two slips of paper and a pencil. Each player writes down one question on one of the papers, and an answer on the other. A player's question and answer do not have to be related at all. In fact, more creative and extremely irrelevant questions and answers fit better to the purposes of the game. The papers are then collected – keeping the questions and answers in separate bundles. Every player picks one question and one answer. Then the pairs of Q and As are read out one by one. At the end of the round, players vote for their favourite match of question–answer. The writers of those question and answer get one point each.

THE QUEUING GAME

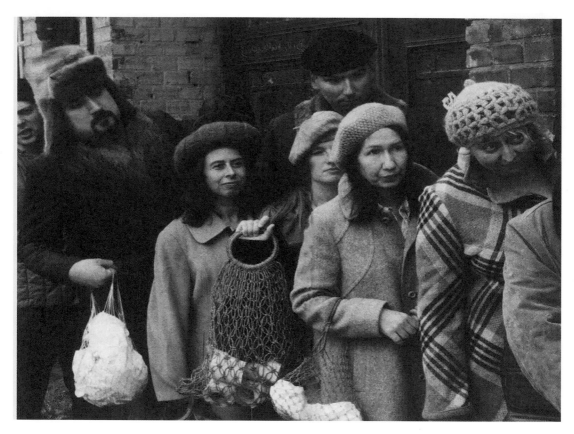

Cards from the Polish game Kolejka (The Queue) in which players join queues to buy goods from shops which are often empty, and to which deliveries are unpredictable. Goods can also be exchanged on the black market. The game was launched in 2011 as an educational tool to teach children what life was like for parents in the communist era.

- LISTA SPOŁECZNA -

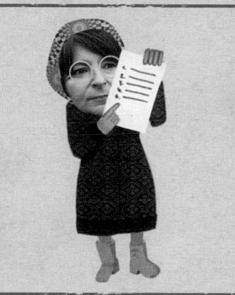

Powstała lista społeczna, uprawniająca
do nowego miejsca w kolejce.

ZŁAP WYBRANĄ KOLEJKĘ W DWA PALCE
I USTAW TYŁ NA PRZÓD, TAK ŻEBY
OSTATNI PIONEK BYŁ PIERWSZY.

- SZCZĘŚLIWY TRAF -

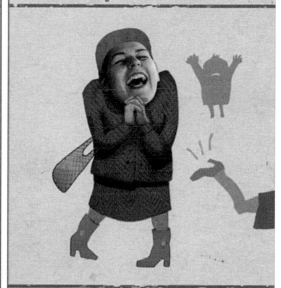

Znajoma musiała odebrać dziecko
z przedszkola i odstąpiła ci swoje
miejsce w kolejce.

PRZESUŃ SWÓJ PIONEK NA DRUGIE
MIEJSCE DO SĄSIEDNIEJ KOLEJKI.

WRITING GAMES

WRITE A SIX-WORD MEMOIR

Ernest Hemingway, challenged to write a short story in only six words, wrote:

For sale. Baby shoes. Never worn.

WRITE A TWITTER STORY

Nicci Gerrard and Sean French, challenged to write a story with only 140 characters, or less, wrote:

Darkness. I woke, felt the familiar weight in the bed, the breathing, the hand on my skin. 'Oh, Paul,' I said. 'Who's Paul?' said the voice.

WRITE TO ORDER

Find someone else to write what you want.

BECOME A PLAGIARIST

Use writing from other people's work.

BECOME AN EAVESDROPPER

Write only what you overhear.

BECOME A SAGE

Blend two sayings to get a new one.
Let's burn that bridge when we come to it

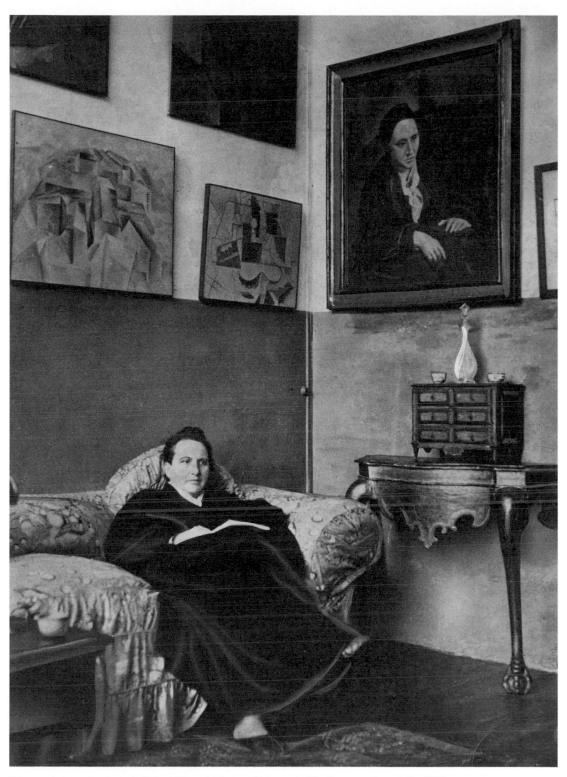

Unknown photographer, Gertrude Stein at 27 rue de Fleurus with her portrait by Picasso on the wall, May 1930

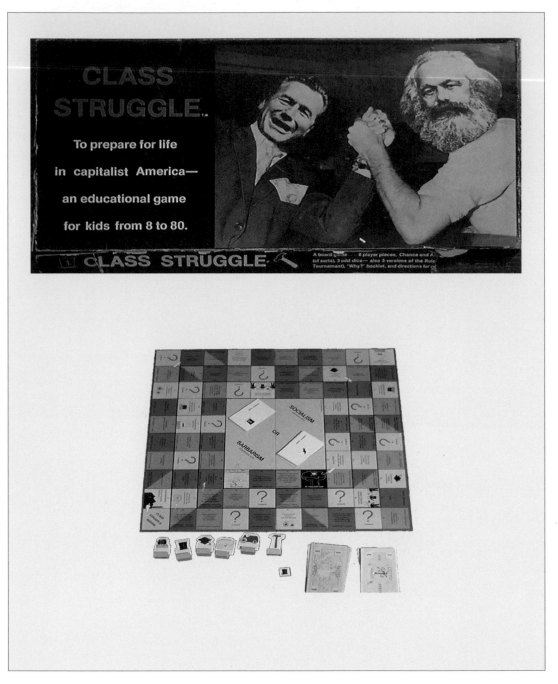

Bertell Ollman's Class Struggle board game (1978) pitted workers against capitalists, represented by hammers and top hats

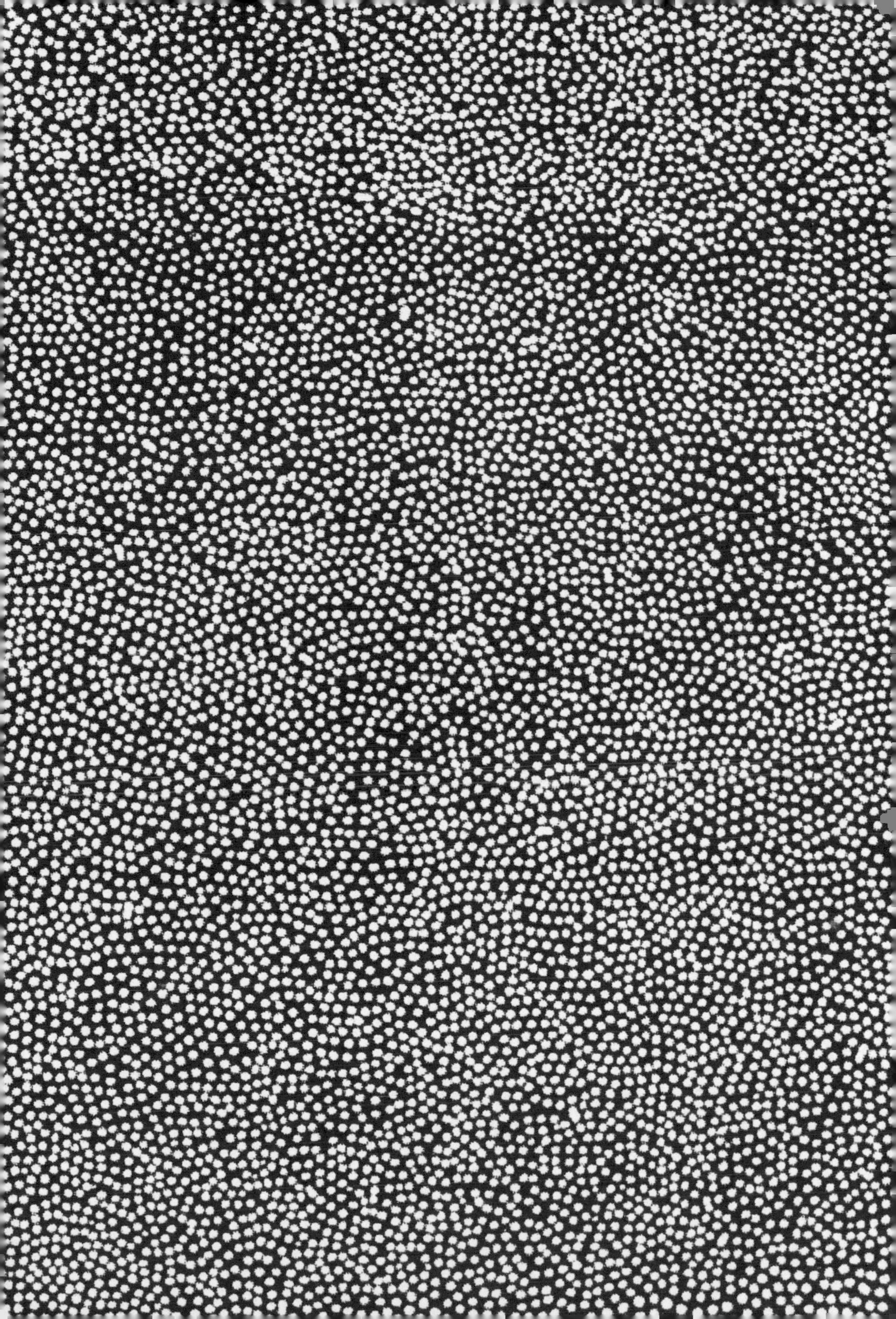

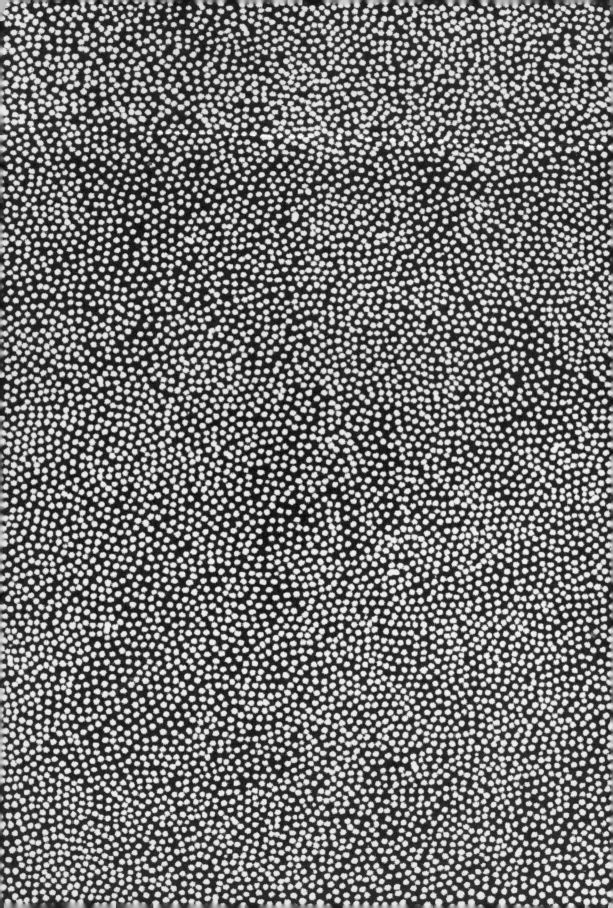

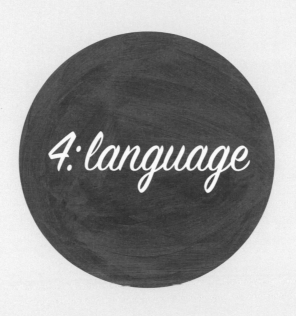

4:language

In language play we can turn the world upside down, say the thing that is not, create impossibilities, defy logic, escape from one reality to another, suspend disbelief. We can talk to friends in private languages: back-slang, polari, lingo, patois. Listening to songs and stories, reading novels, watching films, and in all manner of other activities, we laugh and cry at what has never happened and never will. Magic reality! The philosopher Wittgenstein described what we do when we speak, listen, read, write as 'language games': we play them all the time. Playing them is what makes us human, and very clever with it.

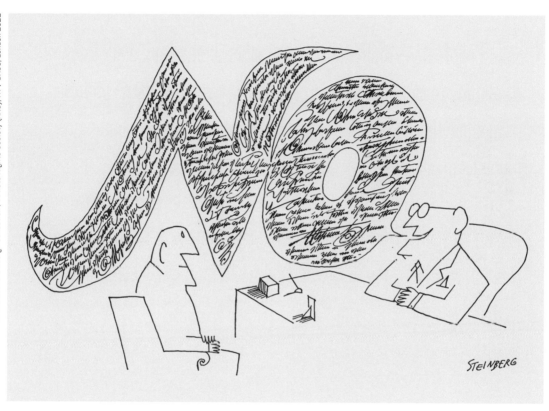

Saul Steinberg, 'Untitled', *New Yorker*, November 25, 1961

fragment: People don't really talk to each other at all. They don't think of something to say, choose the words to express it and then carefully pronounce those words. They use language to disguise meaning as much as to convey it. But other things tell us what they have in mind – and sometimes we have no idea of what they are. I heard myself say, although I could not have said quite how I had acquired this information, "You're saying Paul has a kind of ... secret hideout? Is that what you are saying?" *from a new novel (1997), here anonymous.*

Joseph Kosuth, *Untitled*, 1997

ALEKSANDER DOBA

After his second crossing of the Atlantic, from Portugal to Florida, during which he spent 164 days at sea, Aleksander Doba went to Washington to receive an award from the National Geographic Society as the 2015 People's Choice Adventurer of the Year. Event producers asked him to walk onstage and say, in English, 'Thank you very much.' Doba, who wore jeans to the June ceremony, walked onstage and said,

'Polacy nie gęsi i swój język mają.'

Polish people are not geese and have their own language.

From Elizabeth Weil, 'Alone at Sea', *New York Times*, 2018

GREAT-APE LANGUAGE

A poem written in great-ape language with a translation:

Zor boden tanda	Where are you going, gorilla,
Kagoda bolgani	In the dark forest?
Rak gom tand panda	You run without a sound
Yatokalan mangani	Seeking the female ape.
Kreegh-ah yel greeh-ah	Beware of love
Kreegh-ah zu-vo bolgani	Watch out, gorilla
Greek-ah tand pogo	A lover dies of hunger
Ubor zee kalan mangani	Of thirst, of hoping for the leg of the female great-ape.

The great-ape language has the peculiarity of being composed of a lexicon of less than 300 words. In the absence of any information, it must be deemed that the syntax is according to the user's preference, as are the pronunciation and the prosody.

Jacques Jouet, *The Great-Ape Love-Song* in Raymond Queneau, ed, The Oulipo Laboratory, 1995

SYNONYMS

4/30/80

Making list of words, to thicken my active vocabulary. To have puny, not just little, hoax, not just trick, mortifying, not just embarrassing, bogus, not just fake.

I could make a story out of puny, hoax, mortifying, bogus.

They *are* a story.

From Susan Sontag, *As Consciousness Is Harnessed To Flesh, Diaries 1964–1980*

ENGLISH AS SHE IS SPOKE

In this world of uncertainties, there is, at any rate, one thing which may be pretty confidently set down as a certainty: and that is, that this celebrated little phrase-book will never die while the English language lasts.

Mark Twain (introducing the American edition in 1883)

Senhor Pedro Carolino first published his *New Guide of the Conversation in Portuguese and English* in 1855. Its ineffable absurdity derives from a perfectly logical premise: that it should be possible to compile a text book to a language unknown to the compiler by means of reference works in an intermediary language. Carolino's guide was put together, it must be assumed, using a Portuguese–French phrase book and an English–French dictionary.

The wonderful originality of Carolina's 'English' is not without a strange and surprising poetry of its own, unimaginable without the inadvertent transformations effected by his method. The application of its logic creates a kind of unconscious through which the ordinary and everyday is transmuted into the improbable gold of inspired nonsense.

OF THE MAN	WOMAN OBJECTS	FISHES AND SHELL-FISHES	GAMES
The brain	The busk	Calamary	Foot-ball
The brains	The sash	Dorado	Bar
The fat of the leg	The cornet	A sorte of fish	Gleek
The ham	The pumps	Hedge hog	Carousal
The inferior lip	The paint or disguise	Large lobster	Pile
The superior lip	The patches	Snail	Mall
The marrow	The skate	Wolf	Even or non even

FAMILIAR PHRASES

Go to send for.

Have you say that?

Have you understand that he says?

At what purpose have say so?

Put your confidence at my.

At what o'clock dine him?

Apply you at the study during that you are young.

Dress your hairs:

Wax my shoes.

That is that I have think.

That are the dishes whose you must be and to abstain.

This meat ist not too over do.

This ink is white.

This room is filled of bugs.

This girl have a beauty edge.

It is a noise which to cleave the head.

This wood is fill of thief's.

Tell me, it can one to know?

IDIOTISMS AND PROVERBS

The necessity don't know the low.

Few, few the bird make her nest.

He is not valuable to breat that he eat.

Its are some blu stories.

Nothing some money, nothing of Swiss.

He sin in trouble water.

A bad arrangement is better than a process.

He has a good beak.

In the country of blinds, the one eyed men are kings.

To build castles in Espagnish.

Cat scalded fear the cold water.

To do the fine spirit.

With a tongue one go to Roma.

There is not any ruler without a exception.

Take out the live coals with the hand of the cat.

A horse baared don't look him the tooth.

Take the occasion for the hairs.

To do a wink to some body.

So many go the jar to spring, than at last rest there.

He eat until to can't more.

Which like Bertram, love hir dog.

It want to beat the iron during it is hot.

It is better be single as a bad company.

The stone as roll not heap up not foam.

They shurt him the doar in face.

He has fond the knuckle of the business.

He turns as a weath turcocl.

There is not better sauce who the appetite.

The pains come at horse and turn one's self at foot.

He is beggar as a church rat.

So much go the jar to spring that at last it break there.

To force to forge, becomes smith.

Keep the chestnut of the fire with the cat foot.

Friendship of a child is water into a basket.

At some thing the misforte is good.

Burn the politeness.

Tell me whom thou frequent, I will tell you which you are.

After the paunch comes the dance.

Of the hand to mouth, one lose often the soup.

To look for a needle in a hay bundle.

To craunch the marmoset.

To buy cat in pocket.

She do not that to talk and to cackle.

He laughs at my nose, he jest by me.

He has spit in my coat.

He has me take out my hairs.

He does me some kicks.

He has scratch the face with hers nails.

He burns one's self the brains.

He is valuable his weight's gold.

He has the word for to laugh.

He do the devil at four.

He was fighted in duel.

They fight one's selfs together.

He do want to fall.

It must never to laugh of the unhappies.

He was wanting to be killed.

I am confused all yours civilities.

I am catched cold.

I not make what to cough and spit.

Never I have feeld a such heat.

I have mind to vomit.

SPAIN

CHARLES BOYLE

'Spain' is composed of sentences plucked from *Classified Revision Exercises in Spanish* by E. Hart Dyke, MA, and W. E. Capel Cure, MA — two sentences from the ten in each of thirty exercises designed for the practice of particular constructions ('Adverbs and Conjunctions', 'Reflexives and Reciprocals', etc.). The sentences are units of meaning without context, like snatches of conversation overheard on the bus: begging for narrative connection, and resisting.

He said that truth was the most important thing.
He gave me such a look that I went into another room.

His younger sister is very inquisitive.
A very important thing has just happened.

Philip the Second died on September 13th, 1598.
What time was it when he left? It must have been about 5 am

It's a long time ago that it happened.
In windy weather, one may lose one's hat.

He doesn't like it; nor I either.
I have no books; nor do I want any.

He was not so ugly as his brother.
The task is becoming more and more difficult.

Who is it that is calling us? It is we.
The streets are dirty because it has rained a lot.

Don't do it now; do it later, please.
Don't speak to me in that way; speak to me more politely.

He lost the sword with which he has killed so many enemies.
Which of the sailors came with you?

I have found your handkerchief, but now I have lost mine.
The man with the black beard did this.

Has anyone ever done a thing that seems so stupid?
Let no one come in till six o'clock.

I was looking for a child who could read and write.
Ask him to go off a little way off from the window.

They were unwilling to speak to the others, or for the others to speak to them.
I want you to write to me every week.

If I told you I had done it, would you believe me?
If there is no snow in the mountains, it almost always rains.

It is possible that my brother is the author.
It was not yet certain that there had been a revolution.

As soon as he saw me, he asked when I would go.
Provided he does this, he can take everything.

Whoever he may be, speak to him politely.
Whatever shoes you wear, they must be strong.

Nothing may be said here.
Each man may do as he likes.

Please look for my stick: I should be sorry to lose it.
These oranges must have come from Spain.

They were in the act of doing this when I came in.
As the window was still open, it was shut by the waiter.

When their aunt entered the room, she was told the news.
The dog was seen wandering alone though the town.

We don't love one another, do we?
He was sitting in an armchair, and soon went to sleep.

I spent the afternoon not sleeping, but writing letters.
It would be something to know where we are going to.

Look for him outside; he's not likely to be under the table.
I am tired of working without achieving anything.

I believe he bought this for me, but it will be useless.
There will be no prize for those who can't swim.

He lost half his money in the shipwreck.
These woollen stockings are eighteen inches long.

Would that we had already arrived!
How badly your brother writes!

Having dropped my pen, I can't write any more.
Go up and tell them breakfast is ready.

I have heard they are going to be married next week.
A complete stranger asked me for a cigarette.

He found more books than he had lost.
I insist on this lesson ending now.

ANGST

SYLVIA LIBEDINSKY

If I had to guess the meaning of German words by their sound, this is what I'd say: ANGST: an ancient city in the Arctic, APFELSTRUDEL: a tractor, SCHOPENHAUER: a thick winter soup, PUMPERNICKEL: a circus clown, POLTERGEIST: a heavy raincoat, KARTOFFEL: a boy's name.

I find that to use foreign words in my verses I have to dissociate them from their meaning and consider only their sound. That's easy with foreign words. When verses are read, the words and their meaning are re-united to an unpredictable effect. Of course, I do know these words' real meaning now, as they are widely used loanwords in English. But as I learnt them as an adult, it is easy for me to disconnect from their real meaning. The words I learnt as a child still have unequivocal meanings, they are inseparable from whatever they represent. That's why it is impossible to make this sort of 'poetry' in a language I am familiar with. I did try, many times... and failed dismally.

Apfelstrudel, Dieselmotor
Telefunken Gunther Grass
Schwarzenegger mit Volkswagen
Kaspar Hauser
Bundesbank

Farenheit und Werner Herzog
Sauerkraut mit Bruno Ganz
Schopenhauer Kindergarten
Sigmund Freud
und Haagen Dazs

Meistersinger der Lufthansa
Wolfgang Mozart Hinterland
Walter Gropius Schadenfreude
Pumpernikel
Krankenhaus

Brandenburger mit Kartoffeln
Hansel, Gretel und Fritz Lang
Boris Becker Max von Sydow
Niebelungen
Steffi Graff

Sechs und swanzig meine Liebe
Bitte Bitte was ist das?
Ein Rotweiler mit Alzheimer
Rudolf Steiner
Poltergeist

SPEECH

Simple things
one wants to say
like, what's the day
like, out there –
Who am I

and where.

Robert Creeley, from *Later*, 1979

Place words end to end as dry stones.
Using only local materials, arrange them
sparsely to admit plenty of ventilation.
They will stand among the fiercest winds
and keep the sheep out.

Thomas A. Clark, from *A Still Life*, 1977

FROM *ALICE IN WONDERLAND*

LEWIS CARROLL

'I don't know what you mean by "glory",' Alice said.

Humpty Dumpty smiled contemptuously. 'Of course you don't – till I tell you. I meant "there's a nice
knock-down argument for you!"'

'But "glory" doesn't mean "a nice knock-down argument",' Alice objected.

'When I use a word,' Humpty Dumpty said, in rather a scornful tone, 'it means just what I choose it to mean
– neither more nor less.'

'The question is,' said Alice, 'whether you can make words mean so many different things.'

'The question is', said Humpty Dumpty, 'which is to be master – that's all.'

Alice was too much puzzled to say anything; so after a minute Humpty Dumpty began again. 'They've a
temper, some of them – particularly verbs: they're the proudest – adjectives you can do anything with,
but not verbs – however, I can manage the whole lot of them! Impenetrability! That's what I say!'

'Would you tell me please,' said Alice, 'what that means?'

'Now you talk like a reasonable child,' said Humpty Dumpty, looking very much pleased. 'I meant by
"impenetrability" that we've had enough of that subject, and it would be just as well if you'd mention what
you mean to do next, as I suppose you don't mean to stop here all the rest of your life.'

'That's a great deal to make one word mean,' Alice said in a thoughtful tone.

'When I make a word do a lot of work like that,' said Humpty Dumpty, 'I always pay it extra.'

DEAR WHO GIVES A C**P

LYDIA DAVIS

Dear Who Gives a C**p,

Thank you for the recent shipment, which arrived promptly. I'm glad to have it. I feel good about using recycled toilet paper, even if it does not always tear off the roll neatly and is a little coarse, though we quickly got used to that and may even come to like it. In any case, I would rather suffer a slight discomfort than be complicit in the felling of old-growth trees in Canadian boreal forests merely in order to enjoy virgin toilet paper that is softer and tears more neatly. I also appreciate what you are doing to help supply toilets to people around the world who don't have them. But may I make one request? The first shipment you sent — our first order — came in an 'anonymous' cardboard box, which I preferred. The latest shipment had your company name on it. I find that a little awkward. The name may be amusing to some people, and I don't mind it — or not very much — but it's frankly embarrassing to display in the neighbourhood where I live, and it's certainly not language I would use myself. In fact, the language does seem problematic to me, since it is rude and expresses (though I know you intend it tongue-in-cheek) an attitude of brutal indifference that is all too actually pervasive in the times we are living in. I am sure you will not change your company name, but could you please offer the option of shipping your product in an unidentified box? Also, we like the individual wrapping of the toilet rolls, striped and polka-dotted and in such nice pastel colours. Opening the carton is like opening a box full of gifts. But if you didn't print your company name right in the middle of the paper, we could reuse it for wrapping small presents, even though it would be a little wrinkled since we are opposed on principle to ironing. Wouldn't that fit better with your idea of reusing and recycling paper rather than buying single-use gift wrap? Please consider putting your name in the corner of the wrap, or off to the side. Thank you.
Sincerely.

Lydia Davis, 'Dear Who Gives a C**p', *London Review of Books*, vol. 43, issue 1–7, spring 2021

USEFUL PHRASES

6 WAYS OF CALLING SOMEONE STUPID

The cheese slid off his cracker

The wheel's spinning but the hamster's dead

A few peas short of a casserole

A few fries short of a Happy Meal

An intellect rivalled only by garden tools

Elevator doesn't go all the way to the top floor

6 WAYS OF SAYING NO

I promised to help a friend fold road maps

I've changed the lock on my door and now I can't get out

I prefer to remain an enigma

The man on television told me to stay tuned

My crayons all melted together

I'm being deported

CRATE

FRANCIS PONGE

Halfway between *crib* and *cage* the French language puts *crate*, a simple slatted box for transporting those fruits that fall ill at the least lack of air.

Built in such a way that it can be broken down effortlessly after use, it is never used twice. It is really more perishable than the deliquescing foodstuffs that it carries.

On the corners of streets that lead to the markets, it gleams like white wood without wood's vanity. Still very new, and slightly surprised to find itself in this awkward position, having been thrown into the gutter without hope of retrieval, it remains a most likable object on whose fate we will not dwell for long.

From *Partisan of Things*, translated from the French by Joshua Corey and Jean-Luc Garneau, 2016

IMMORTALITY

DAGHULL HAMMETT

I know little of science or art or finance or adventure. I have never written anything except brief and infrequent letters to my sister in Sacramento. My name, were it not painted on the windows of my shop, would be unknown to even the Polish family that lives and has many children across the street. Yet I shall live in the memories of men when those names are on every one's lips now are forgotten, and when the events of today are dim. I do not know whether I shall be remembered as a great wit, a dreamer of strange dreams, a great thinker, or a philosopher; but I do know that I, Oscar Blichy, the grocer, shall be an immortal. I have saved nearly seventeen thousand dollars from the profits of my shop during the last twenty years. I shall add to this amount as much as I can until the day of my death, and then it is to go to the writer of the best biography of me!

From Daghull Hammett, *10 Story Book*, 1922. Daghull Hammett was the pen name of Dashiell Hammett

MEMOIRS OF A PUDDLE

ISTVÁN ÖRKÉNY

It rained all day on March 22nd, 1972 and I collected myself in a very delectable place. I might as well give the exact location: in front of No. 7 Dráva Street, Budapest, 13th district, where there is a pothole in the pavement.

I was living there, ticking over. Many a man stepped into me, then looking back they cursed me, swore at me, and used harsh words which I am loath to repeat.

I was a puddle for two days, taking the insults lying down. It is common knowledge that the sun shone again on the 24th. Oh, the paradoxes of life! I dried up when the weather turned fine!

What else shall I say? Did I do all right? Did I make a fool of myself? Did I perhaps fall short of the expectations of the people at 7 Dráva Street? Not that it makes any difference, really, but all the same it would be nice to know, if only because after me puddles will go on collecting there. We live fast, our days are numbered, and while I was spending my days down there, a new generation sprang up, vigorous and ready for action, all of them ambitious potential puddles and they bothered me with importunate questions as to what they might expect in that promising pothole.

But all in all I 'puddled' for a bare two days and all that this allows me to say is that the tone of life is abusive; that Dráva Street is damned windy; and that the sun is forever shining when it has no business to, but at least you don't have to trickle down the drain pipe. Oh boys, what holes, what depressions! Bursting pipes! Sagging roads! These are great things nowadays! All you young people, listen to me, forward to Dráva Street!

From *One-Minute Stories*, translated by László I. András, 1995

IMPROVING MY GERMAN

LYDIA DAVIS

All my life I have been trying to improve my German.

At last my German is better.

— But now I am old and ill and don't have long to live.

Soon I will be dead,

With better German.

First published in *Paris Review*, issue 234, autumn 2020

LONDON

SOPHIE HERXHEIMER

*A poem told in the voice of the author's
German Jewish grandmother (to be read aloud)*

Not zo mainy Dais zinz ve arrivink.
Zis grey iss like Bearlin, zis same grey Day
ve hef. Zis norzern Vezzer, oont ze demp Street.
A biet off Rain voant hurt, vill help ze Treez
on zis Hempstet Heese ve see in Fekt.
Vy shootd I mind zat?

I try viz ze Busses, Her Kondooktor eskink
me ... for vot? I don't eckzectly rememober,
Fess plees? To him, my Penny I hent ofa—
He notdz viz a keint Smile – *Fanks Luv!*
He sez. Oh! I em his Luff – turns Hentell
on Machine, out kurls a Tikett.

Zis is ven I know zat here to settle iss OK. Zis
City vill be Home, verr eefen on ze Buss is Luff.

From *Velkom to Inklandt*, 2017

FROM *A FEW TOO MANY*

JOAN ACOCELLA

Some words for hangover, like ours, refer prosaically to the cause: the Egyptians say they are 'still drunk', the Japanese 'two days drunk', the Chinese 'drunk overnight', The Swedes get 'smacked from behind'. But it is in languages that describe the effects rather than the cause that we begin to see real poetic power. Salvadorans wake up 'made of rubber', the French with a 'wooden mouth' or a 'hair ache', The Germans and the Dutch say they have a 'tomcat', presumably wailing. The Poles, reportedly, experience a 'howling of kittens'. My favourites are the Danes, who get 'carpenters in the forehead'. In keeping with the saying about the Eskimos' nine words for snow, the Ukrainians have several words for hangover. And, in keeping with the Jews-don't-drink-rule, Hebrew didn't even have one word until recently. Then the experts at the Academy of the Hebrew Language, in Tel Aviv, decided that such a term was needed, so they made one up: *hamarmoret*, derived from the word for fermentation. (Hamarmoret echoes a usage of Jeremiah's, in Lamentations 1:20, which the King James Bible translates as 'my bowels are troubled'.)

New Yorker, 2008

FROM *THE BEST OF MYLES*

MYLES NA GOPALEEN

ABSINTHE MAKES THE HEART GROW WARMER

WAITER, what was in that glass?

Arsenic, sir.

ARSENIC. I asked you to bring me absinthe.

I thought you said arsenic. I beg your pardon, Sir.

Do you realise what you've done, you clumsy fool? I'm dying.

I am extremely sorry, Sir.

I DISTINCTLY SAID ABSINTHE.

I realise that I owe you an apology, sir. I am extremely sorry.

Myles Na Gopaleen was the pen name of Flann O'Brien

FROM *MY LAST BREATH*

LUIS BUNUEL

A peña is a kind of meeting that takes place regularly in certain cafés; it's a tradition that's played a major role in Spanish life, and not only for the literati. People meet according to their profession, and always in the same place, from three to five in the afternoon, or after nine in the evening ... In the political peña at the Café de Platerias, you might meet Sam Blancar, for example, an anarchist from Aragón who wrote for a variety of journals, such as *España Nueva*. His articles were so notoriously extreme that he was automatically arrested the day after any assassination. Then there was Santolaria, who edited a journal with anarchist leanings in Sevilla. There was also Eugenio d'Ors, and the bizarre, magnificent poet Pedro Garfias, who could spend two weeks looking for the right adjective.

'So ... your adjective?' I used to ask whenever we met. 'Have you found it yet?'

'Still looking,' he'd reply dreamily, before drifting off.

1984

FROM *ANIMAL CRACKERS*

GROUCHO MARX

Hello, I must be going

I cannot stay

I came to say

I must be going

I'm glad I came

But just the same

I must be going, la-la!

Captain Spaulding, 1930

INDEX

A NOTE ON CONTRIBUTORS

Mel Gooding wrote the short, sharp introductions to the four sections. Will Hobson contributed generously after many days exploring the London Library. David Bellingham was a brilliant and tireless researcher.
Sally O'Reilly, Philip Terry, Peter Blegvad and Nina Katchadourian all improved the book in different ways.

Many thanks also to: Glen Baxter, Sian Bonnell, Charles Boyle, Anne Clarke, Adam Dant, Mary Dean, Rose Dempsey, Nicci Gerrard, Francis Gooding, Leo Hollis, Hiang Kee, David Nathan-Maister, Cornelia Parker, Lucien Rothenstein, Ella Rothenstein, Ed Ruscha, Ian Sansom, David Shrigley, Mimi Thompson, Shelley Wanger and Carey Young.

First published in 2022
by Redstone Press, 7a St Lawrence Terrace, London W10 5SU
email: redstone.press@gmail.com website: www.theredstoneshop.com

Design: Julian Rothenstein
Artwork: Tom Baxter
Copy editing: Natalie Hume
Production: Geoff Barlow
Printed and bound in China by 1010 Printing International Ltd

Compilation © Redstone Press 2022
Foreword © Andrey Kurkov 2022

ISBN 978-0-9955181-8-6

Distributed worldwide excluding the UK by
ARTBOOK I D.A.P.
75 Broad Street, Suite 630, New York, NY 10004
artbook.com

CREDITS
27: Extract from 'W. H. Auden: A Biography' © Humphrey Carpenter, 1981. Reproduced by permission of
Felicity Bryan Literary Agency and The Estate of Humphrey Carpenter
61: Romuald Hazoumè, 'Azonto', 2016, found object, plastic, synthetic fabric and fibres, 2016
85: Richard Prince, 'The Catcher in the Rye', New York City, USA: American Place, 2011 (unpaginated),
5.5 x 8", hardcover with dust jacket. Edition of 500.
94: Harland Miller, 'The Me I Never Knew', 2018, hand-finished print, 125 x 99.5 cm
95: Harland Miller, 'Painting for Charles Addams', 2012, oil on canvas, 276 x 183 cm
97: Nina Katchadourian, 'Am I Too Loud?', from the series 'Special Collections Revisited' (1996/2008) from the
'Sorted Books' project, 1993 and ongoing. C-print, 12 x 19 inches. 'A Day at the Beach' from the series 'Sorting Shark'
(2001), from the 'Sorted Books' project, 1993 and ongoing. C-print, 12 x 19 inches
110: 'Art Class Assignments' © John Baldessari. Courtesy Estate of John Baldessari
135: Maurizio Cattelan, 'Stadium', wood, acrylic, steel, paper and plastic, 100 cm x 651 cm x 120 cm
158: 'The Collected Poems of Robert Creeley', 1975–2005, by Robert Creeley, © 2006 by the Estate of Robert Creeley
Published by the University of California Press
160: 'Improving My German' and 'Dear Who Gives a C**p' reproduced by permission of Greene & Heaton Ltd
165 Sophie Herxheimer, 'Velkom to Inklandt', courtesy Short Books